A Billion Voices

A Billion Voices

A journey through the bizarre, the chaotic, the exquisite, the anarchic, the little known side of India

Phillip Adams

ABC BOOKS

To Annabelle, who willed it.

To Sandra, who typed it.

To Susan, who read it.

Published by ABC Books for the
AUSTRALIAN BROADCASTING CORPORATION
GPO Box 9994 Sydney NSW 2001

Copyright © Phillip Adams 1999

First published March 1999

All rights reserved. No part of this publication
may be reproduced, stored in a retrieval system
or transmitted in any form or by any means,
electronic, mechanical photocopying, recording
or otherwise, without the prior written permission
of the Australian Broadcasting Corporation.

National Library of Australia
Cataloguing-in-Publication entry
Adams, Phillip, 1939-.
    A billion voices : a journey through the bizarre, the
    chaotic, the exquisite, the anarchic, the little known side
    of India.

    ISBN 0 7333 0707 8.

    1. Adams, Phillip, 1939- –Journeys –India. 2. India –
    Description and travel. 1 Title.

915 404

Designed by Eckermann Art & Design
Cover by Reno Design Group
Cover photographs by Jane Cavanough and Phillip Adams

Set in 11/14 pt Tiepolo by Eckermann Art & Design
Colour separations by Finsbury, Adelaide
Printed and bound in Australia by
Australian Print Group, Maryborough, Victoria

5 4 3 2 1

Contents

Acknowledgments	7
Map of journey across India	8
Introduction	9
1 The Train	13
2 Mumbai	29
3 Gandhi	43
4 The Untouchables	50
5 Poverty	62
6 Mickey Spillane	79
7 Son of Cochise	98
8 Varanasi	106
9 Calcutta	128
10 Astrologers	144
11 Cemeteries	154
12 How to Achieve Serenity in the Slammer	165
13 Suicide in India's Sweden	171
14 Keepers of the Flame	175
15 The Homogenisation of India	197
16 The Bomb	210
17 Conclusion	220

Acknowledgments

The author and publishers would like to thank the Australian-India Council, the Australian High Commission in New Dehli (especially Susan Grace), Jasleen Dhamija, P. Sainath, the staff of the ABC Bureau in New Dehli, and Radio National.

The author and publishers gratefully acknowledge the following sources from which quoted material has been drawn:

Robert Jungk, *Brighter Than 1000 Suns*, Harcourt Brace, USA

Arundhati Roy, *The God of Small Things*, Harper Collins, UK

Shashi Tharoor, *The Great Indian Novel*, Picador UK

Atal Bihari Vajpayee, 'Hiroshima ki Peedha' from *My 51 Poems*, translation by P. Sainath

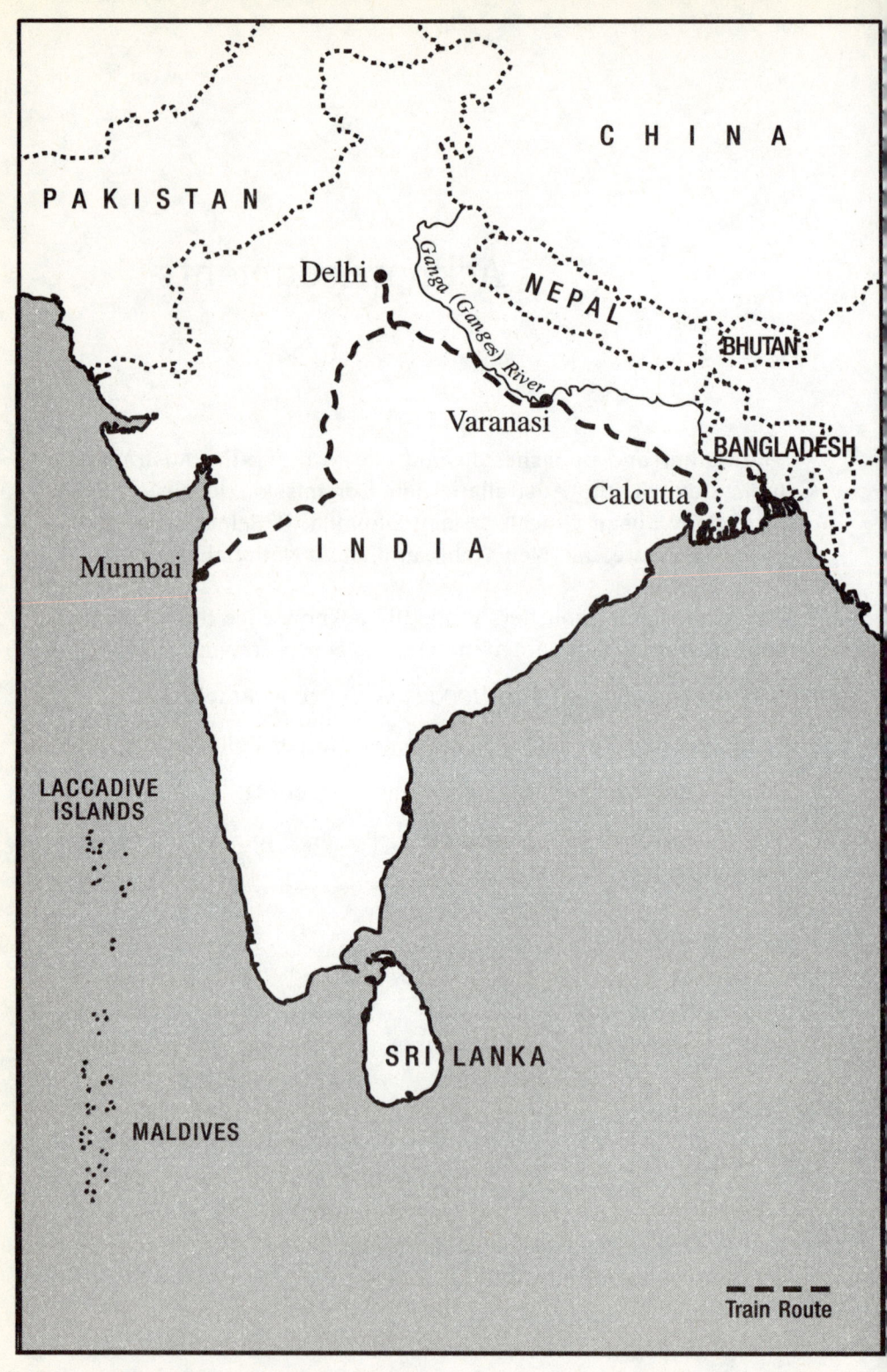

Introduction

The many cultures of India pass through each other like shafts of coloured light. You have a glimmering of the quantum mechanical notion of the parallel universe. For in India, entire cosmologies, neither colliding nor blending, simply occupy the same space.

Arundhati Roy writes of the 'vast, violent, circling, driving, ridiculous, insane, unfeasible public turmoil' of the nation. That is far too serene, too calm a description of India's reality, totality, insanity. This isn't a nation so much as a glorious mess, a chaos of theories and theologies.

Defying analysis and defeating description, India is like the old story, presumably Indian in origin, of the blind men and the elephant. Feel its tail and the creature is like a rope. Touch its belly and it's like a great barrel. A leg? An elephant is like a tree. So what hope have we with the great painted pachyderm of India? A trunk, a tusk, a flapping ear, a wrinkled skin, a great head ablaze with pattern and colour. Every encounter with India defeats every scholar, every political analyst, every theologian, every demographer. Finally it's a nonsense to talk about India. There is no India. And every time I visit I know less about it.

But to be honest, I also fail to understand Australia. The dynamics revealed in recent elections make that painfully obvious. One Nation released old bigotries that spread across the landscape like prickly pear, hopping across it like cane toads, covering the great coral reef of multiculturalism with the Crown of Thorns of Hansonism. I thought we were beyond that — that we'd learnt to celebrate diversity.

Oops.

Compared to India, Australian society is simplicity itself.

We are eighteen million people occupying one of the world's largest slabs of real estate. Leaving aside the plight of our Indigenous people (something we've always found quite easy to do), our social problems rate about one on the Richter Scale. Not merely well fed we're overfed, many spending more money on dieting than entire Indian families, perhaps villages, spend on food. Our newsagencies groan beneath the weight of magazines that are full of methods by which we can cut thousands of kilojoules from every meal, whereas hundreds of millions of Indians cannot scrape together 2000 calories a day.

Australia is wealthy beyond the dreams of avarice, our population as well educated as any in history, and floods, droughts and bushfires notwithstanding, we live in a land where Mother Nature behaves more like a Christian saint than one of those destructive Hindu deities. Yet despite our manifold blessings, we are increasingly a nation of grizzlers, having replaced the cultural cringe with the culture of complaint. If belly-aching was an Olympic event, we'd be guaranteed Gold at Sydney in the year 2000.

A nation ruled by top politicians in thrall to shock-jocks and public opinion polls, Australia is in no position to patronise the world's biggest democracy, or to belittle its achievements. A billion people are, despite immense obstacles, making a go of it. And while a third of that population endures apocalyptic poverty, the mass starvation that was common under British rule has disappeared.

In Australia, the notion of cultural integrity is becoming oxymoronic, whereas, thus far, India has managed to hybridise global influences. Indian film, television and popular music may be increasingly a mishmash but the flavour of their culture, far stronger than any curry, still dominates. Nor can we criticise India for its racial and religious conflicts. Not when ours are escalating, when we seem to be surrendering to the proud traditions of the White Australia Policy.

As I travelled India with my colleagues Annabelle Quince,

Jane Cavanough and Donna McLachlan, I found that we were not alone in our bedazzled befuddlement. We learnt that the editors of the great Indian newspapers are as nonplussed as the politicians. While the gurus and the academics feign wisdom, and the all-seeing novelists can be immensely perceptive, at best, each of them possesses just one or two pieces of a puzzle, of a jiggling, ever-changing jigsaw. And no sooner do a couple of shapes seem to fit together with apparent snugness than you realise you've got it wrong.

Travelling for a reason is the best way to travel. Travelling with a purpose. If you're lugging a camera or tape recorder or even brandishing a notebook you can get to talk to people. Get into their offices. Their homes. I've often thought I should always travel with a prosthetic tape recorder or video camera, just a casing without any guts. With a couple of lights that flash. So I could do fake interviews.

In fact, I did fake interviews when making a documentary in Egypt with Paul Cox. We were always in trouble with the Egyptian bureaucracy when we were filming around the digs at Saqqara. And the way to calm everyone down, to smooth everyone over, was either to bribe or do an interview. And interviews, particularly fake interviews, were cheaper. So I'd meander around the Step pyramid with a big cheese from the Antiquities Department, asking questions while the camera operator staggered backwards over the broken ground and the sound recordist pointed his microphone, in its woolly jumper. Thereafter difficulties with permits would vanish. The bureaucrat would beam with pleasure at the thought of being on television.

On this trip the interviews were authentic. We talked to Untouchables on the burning *ghats*, to aristocratic Parsis, to holy men, to young filmmakers, to belligerent new ministers in the BJP government, to novelists, to venerated scholars, to the President himself. Nevertheless, the jigsaw refused to form a coherent picture.

As ever I returned home with curiosity unsatisfied and intensified. That's all I can offer with this little book, but at the end of it you'll want to know more about India — a nation that will soon be as populous as China. A nation that demands to be taken seriously.

1

The Train

To be in a major Indian city is to be surrounded by the population of Beijing, the energy of New York, the traditions of London and the antiquity of Rome. But first and foremost, it is to be overwhelmed by the immensity and intensity of Indianness.

After a couple of hours on the streets of India you can't see any more. You're blind from looking. You have to close your eyes if you're to remember something, let alone comprehend it, from the maelstrom.

We're at Bombay station. Bombay, the name by which I've always known this city. But in January 1996, it was changed to Mumbai, after the goddess worshipped by the original inhabitants. 'Bombay' was a Portuguese corruption of her name. Now we're in a train compartment, at the beginning of a journey that will take us across half a dozen states and 1300 kilometres, to Delhi. In the next fourteen hours we'll have an experience that will blend four of the dominant ingredients in Indian life: the railway, the cinema, the bureaucracy, the anarchy.

Indians describe India as a land of a billion anarchists. Yet there seems to be an equal number of bureaucrats. The entire nation is locked in an endless conflict between spontaneity and rigidity, between creative chaos and the claustrophobic of regulation. But perhaps the anarchists are winning.

Mumbai station, one of India's vast temples to the train, as preposterous a celebration of metal as Eiffel's Tower or Sydney's Harbour Bridge, embraces perhaps 10,000 jostling, demanding, yearning individuals, each and every one of them at war with the by-laws.

It would have been easier if we'd lugged the luggage ourselves, through crowds of improbable density, struggling up and down Everests of stairs, than to have dealt with the porters who fought us, and each other, for possession of suitcases, tripods, sound gear. Now we've laid claim to the compartments designated on our tickets but will soon find that the relationship between reservation and seat is tenuous, and will spend much of the journey repelling boarders from our bunks. For the moment, though, there's something like peace.

Outside, the teeming millions of India are, as advertised, teeming. But not teaming. Despite the classifications of caste, despite the rules and regulations, the billion Indians refuse to be regulated and are, most emphatically, not ant-like. The bruising bustle is made up entirely of individuals. Thus the local teamsters, the luggage wallahs, are engaged in constant internecine squabbling. Although they're dues-paying members of a union every bag provokes a deafening demarcation dispute.

It's the same with Mumbai's great bounty of beggars. Not for them anonymity, let alone fraternity. You are forever confronted by a singular human being, someone with urgent hands (or stumps, as the case may be) and inescapable eyes. People in India refuse to be statistics. They insist on being as real, as emphatic, as yourself.

Pushing through the crowds I remembered the terrors I felt as a child when a science teacher, aided and abetted by chalk on blackboard, described a future where human beings, faster breeding than any nuclear reactor, would reach a critical mass by the end of the century, which would have the entire planet packed with humans shoulder-to-shoulder, standing stiffly erect and suffocating in their own fecundity. Well, here is that future, alive and kicking. And it's not entirely unpleasant. It exhilarates as well as exhausts. Nonetheless, it's good to sink back into what one foolishly imagines to be the sanctity of a reserved seat.

A suburban train, packed to the gunwales, arrives at the next platform. The most crowded carriages are allocated to the tiffin-wallahs, members of a profession that dates back to the earliest days of the Raj. They make this trip every day, carrying hot meals for business executives in Mumbai's CBD — fish, curry, rice and pickles, cooked by mum, wife or servant back home. The meals have been collected from the door and carried to the local railway station by bike, billycart or bonk-borne basket. Now 6000 tiffin-wallahs will deliver the lunches to hundreds of thousands of clients up and down Mahatma Gandhi Road and its posh tributaries, charging them no more than a dollar a week. As long as they remain fleet of foot the fast-food franchises will be held at bay.

In a cinema, the curtains part to reveal the screen. In my train, as the carriage creaks into slow-motion, I pulled the curtain aside myself. And the show begins.

This train, any train, is a cinema on wheels. The sound of the carriage riding the rails, clacking over the sleepers, recalls the slap of film on sprockets as it spools through a projector. Your window, your screen, provides a moving panorama of drama and longueur, of a world that seems close enough to touch. But in neither train nor cinema can you touch, or smell.

You view the world at an interesting angle from the front stalls of a train. The world presents its face to the road and its behind to the railway tracks. In a car you see the facades of houses, public buildings, factories. From the train you see the junk in the backyards, the dirty secrets of the industrial process.

I look down at the parallel tracks. It's like watching film footage race through an editing machine, a Steenbeck or Moviola. And I recall cinema's long affinity with trains.

A few years ago, Barry Cohen, as Minister for the Arts, Heritage and Lost Causes, was announcing the nominees for the AFI Awards. He got to the Best Director and named, as the first of the bunch, Bob Ellis, for his *Warm Nights on a Slow Moving Train*. But the minister got it wrong. *Warm Tights on a Slow Moving Train*, he said. Given the erotic pretensions of Ellis's film, there was delighted laughter from the throng.

On the Mumbai to Delhi journey we keep revising the Ellis title. *Strange Sights on a Slow Moving Train, Warm Bites on a Slow Moving Train, Hot Fights on a Slow Moving Train.*

Decades before Alfred Hitchcock, among others, began using

the train pornographically — with engines plunging into tunnels a metaphor for penetration — the train had been a train of thought for filmmakers. At the first public screening of projected motion film, the Lumiere brothers, Louis and Auguste, thrilled their Parisian audience to the point of panic with the image of a steam engine arriving at a platform. Meanwhile, in New York, people were sitting in train carriages that were mechanically rocked, while moving scenery was projected on the windows.

Mumbai was a small trading post under the Portuguese. It passed into British possession as a consequence of the restoration of Charles II when he married the Portuguese princess Catherine of Braganza in 1662; it was part of her dowry. Playing second fiddle to Calcutta for centuries, it became India's chief port when the Suez Canal was opened in 1869 — the trading centre for raw cotton and silk, for ivory and inlay work, and for opium.

Not so much opium is smoked these days. How could it compete with the pollution?

During the First World War the Brits encouraged Bombay's financiers to build factories to supply the need for textiles. So the city became a monsoonal Lancashire, drawing landless peasants from the rural areas into its workforce. The mill workers became the leaders of the Indian Labour Movement. In a few short years the population rocketed from 800,000 to 13 million. Now real estate prices are stratospheric — the price of land equals that of New York or Tokyo. Mumbai's population density is over 17,000 per square kilometre, nudging New York's, greater than Beijing. Fifty-five per cent of the people live in shanties, slums and on the pavements; living cheek-by-jowl with the very rich. Is there anywhere else on Earth where the contrast between poverty and wealth is as stark?

Of course there is. There is New York where, on one side of Central Park, people luxuriate in apartments costing tens of millions. While a few blocks away, in Harlem, the most common cause of infant mortality is rat bite in the cradle.

Come to think of it, the contrast between poverty and wealth is becoming stark everywhere. Tony Blair presides over the post-Thatcherite landscape where young merchant bankers complain of being hassled and hustled by people who live in cardboard boxes. Perhaps that's half the fun: you only feel truly rich when you are envied, and threatened, by the poor.

Or served by them. The epicentre of poverty in Mumbai is Sanjay Gandhi Nagar where the population was pushed and shoved by the power brokers of the city, where the people lived in fear of their new homes, built from junk, being bulldozed by the municipal authorities. But gradually a community established itself, helped by a German development agency which handed out basic building materials, allowing many of the shanties to be upgraded into one-storey concrete and plaster homes. And within the oppressive density of the slum political consciousness has been growing, albeit dulled by the widespread addiction to daru liquor, a home brew that no one in Sanjay Gandhi Nagar makes but is enthusiastically imported from outside.

Every day countless thousands of people catch the train into Mumbai, to serve the wealthy, to get the crumbs from the table. But others have found the train journeys too exhausting, too expensive, and have returned to the pavements of Colaba or the slums of Mumbai Central.

We are gliding past the slums of Mumbai that serve, faithfully, the interests of the rich. On the one hand, the rich deplore them. On the other, they quarry the slums for cheap labour. They use them, quite literally, to keep their servants off the street. Throughout Mumbai you hear the rich protesting the injustice of it all. But the bottom line is simply this: to get servants for a few cents a day you must have slums.

The most fortunate of Mumbai — and the city now boasts an extraordinary number of millionaires — despise the slums the way wealthy people everywhere have always despised them, characterising their populations as criminals, prostitutes, thieves. But there's another view, far more legitimate, that sees the slums as containing communities of people who work hard for their families and whose endurance is nothing short of inspirational. 'Slum' might be an appropriate term for the acres of shanties, but the word tells us very little of the aspirations and achievements of the people who live in them.

A mosque slides by, squashed between two factories. From the chimneys black smoke belches, from the minaret, a call to prayer. Huge black oxen wallow in feedlots, in their own shit. Yet they're better housed and better fed than the human beings who take their place in this endless succession of images — in the left-to-right movement that streams past the window. A vision, a Panavision, without limits, without end.

Markets fringe the railway lines and fill the sidings. There are people living in and on the rubbish that is swept from stationary trains. We pass a sign saying 'THE RAILWAYS VERSUS DIRT — WHICH SIDE ARE YOU ON?'. That battle has been long lost and the people are on the side of the rubbish. It provides their nourishment, their shelter, their roofing, their walls, their furniture, their living. Such as it is.

So this is what a 'billion people' means. A vast ejaculation of life. It seems that every sexual act has ended in conception and every conception in birth. More than that, it's as if every single sperm has found an ovum. The mind blurs at the thought of a billion, surrenders to statistics. Is it 100 million below the poverty line? Or 300 million? It depends on where you draw the line.

And the line, in India, is drawn on calorific intake. On that and that alone. If you don't get 2100 calories a day, you're poor. If you do, you're not.

The facts and figures published in government handbooks vanish in the face of a human being. When you look that person in the eye. Or a person looks in yours, while you're trying to avoid the implications of the gaze. As you do with the beggars, the beggars by the thousands, the beggars that touch your arm at every traffic light, or touch the cuff of your trousers while you stand on a railway platform. And you look down and see a legless human on a trolley, or someone splayed out like a creature in a cartoon who's been run over by a steamroller. Each and every one of them is a human being and 'nothing that is human is alien to me'. I was haunted by those words when, as a kid, I leafed through the pages of *The Family of Man*, a remarkable collection of photographs accompanied by quotations from poetry, fiction, sacred texts.

Well, here's the family of man. In your face. But, for the time being, they're safely on the other side of the screen. They're in the movie and you're in the audience. Whereas in Mumbai we were all in the crowd of extras.

The train is gliding, sliding, chiding. How can you bear to

be a member of the human race that allows the atrocity of profound poverty to be perpetrated on your fellow beings? How can anybody do anything, how can people waste their time on any other cause or issue, that doesn't address the problems of population and poverty? Which are, of course, adjacent, parallel, like the railway lines.

More painted signs, like Val Morgan slides in the cinema. The ads for thongs and shows are no longer in English but in Hindi or Muslim script. We're ambling through the shambling landscape. Now, as we pick up speed, there's a relief from the close-ups of poverty — we see mud flats and mangroves which, in turn, bring us to rivers. At first sight I assume that people are planting rice in paddies. But no, they're harvesting salt. The paddies are designed to evaporate the brackish water. Salt: the great Indian metaphor. It was the business that the British controlled ruthlessly and that Gandhi dared to challenge in his famous walk to the ocean. What tea was to the Bostonians in their harbour, salt was to Gandhi and his freedom marchers.

The film unfurls. There are fish traps in dams that are little more than puddles. Women collecting water from cement-lined wells, plonking buckets and bowls on their heads. Here women will carry 40, 50 kilos of wood in this way — at least their own weight. Or a man will load sacks of coal (coal which has been illegally removed from the fringes of the coalmine, coal that nobody wants but that, officially, nobody can have) and dangle them on his battered bicycle. If we tried, we might push the bike 100 metres but he'll wheel that load 40 kilometres and get paid a dollar if he's lucky.

The train is powered by diesel. On my previous trips to India, the rails trembled to the stentorian huffings and puffings of steam. India was a great train set beloved of the trainspotters of the world who would arrive with cameras so that the engines could be remembered on Kodachrome, their vital statistics recorded in notebooks. Now the monsters are abandoned in the shunting yards or have been dismantled for scrap. And with them went perhaps 100,000 jobs. Not the least of them being the least of them — the women who raked through the smouldering detritus in the tinder boxes, picking out pieces of unburnt coal with deft movements of darkened fingers. It was another profession frowned upon by the bureaucracy, but the women retrieved enough coal to make a living. So they are the latest victims of progress. And there are many victims of progress in India.

There was a similar loss of employment when Calcutta banned rickshaws. The symbolism was fine but the economic consequences were disastrous for people who'd earned their living pulling symbols of colonial oppression. There was nothing left for them but to join the ranks of the beggars.

Behold the outskirts of Mumbai, through a train window. Darkly. The window is dirty and streaked, like the drive-in screens I remember from the 1950s that muddied projected skies and blotched the unblemished complexions of movie stars. Now the train proceeds at walking pace and I'm in the front stalls gazing at close-ups of the lives of countless people. Here a couple of kids play cards, using a surplus railway sleeper as their table; the train tracks are the nearest thing they have to a playground. And here a man squats to defecate. Is he indifferent to our proximity or hostile to it? Or perhaps he's a social critic, telling the world what he thinks of first class passengers.

I wonder why nobody returns my gaze, later discovering that the train's windows are coated in reflective film. Like a witness looking through mirrored glass at a police line-up, I have the advantage.

The train gains pace, providing a continuous crab-dolly shot, one that will show me a nation. As in a cinema, the screen will be filled with motion and commotion while I sit motionless in the audience. But not emotionless. Although I won't feel the pain of living in poverty, I'll be able to experience the safe, facile feelings that come with a ticket purchased at the box office. Or on a railway platform.

The poverty smacks you in the face. It overwhelms. There is no wasteland; every scrap is occupied by a home, a bed, a vegetable garden, an advertising sign. These have been hand-painted in virulent colours along the walls facing the railway line. They're crudely painted; New York graffiti is far more sophisticated. So the signwriters have produced Reeboks that look more like cars while the cars look like Reeboks. There are ads for *2001: a Space Odyssey*, dating back to the 1970s, when 2001 was a lifetime away. The signs have been defaced by official defacers, presumably because they either haven't been paid for or because the rental has run out. But the defacement only increases the graphic impact. You try to read what's underneath the obliterating pigment and, by and large, succeed. That's the trouble with people who deface advertisements, like censorship of any sort it's almost invariably counter-productive. Censorship tends to help the censored.

There's an old Barry McKenzie comic by Barry Humphries and Nicholas Garland which had Bazza hired to scrawl obscenities on posters in the London Underground. The logic was simple. The obscenities drew attention to what was being advertised. The story resonated with me because, down the track, attempts to ban our film version of *Barry McKenzie* would backfire and create a cult. The censor can be the artist's friend.

The train pushes through air which is full of the foul fragrances of industrial pollution. It is so bad that you cannot help but admire the mosquitoes that, having survived its toxicity, continue to spread malaria. Over the years hundreds died and thousands suffered from gas leaks, while the flow of untreated sewage into coastal waters and ground waters ensured spectacular levels of gastroenteritis.

In the time we spend in India I'll glimpse a thousand cricket matches. Any slice of open space — by a school, in a cemetery — will provide a pitch. Here children are playing on a mud flat. They're using a couple of pieces of bamboo for a wicket. Dark limbs as calligraphy in the bright light, recalling the starkness of the cricketers in Drysdale's iconic painting. And I'm reminded that the Australian Test team is in India at the moment. Few people ask me about them, which is fortunate because I know less about cricket than I do about the mysteries of quantum mechanics or rock music.

A woman in a yellow sari walks along a path towards the railway track. Our motion animates her path, so that it crosses the screen like a windscreen wiper. I remember Kate Winslet posing on the prow of the doomed *Titanic*, her outstretched arms like wings, to be revolved through 180 degrees by a computer program.

Waste land. Wasteland. Rusty wheels and axles from scrapped trains lie between the rails and the rice fields. They're everywhere, like the weights of departed weightlifters. And there are any number of half-built buildings retreating into ruins, major projects that have been mysteriously abandoned. What are they? What were they? Private developments that ran out of puff? Foreign aid projects that ran out of funds?

Tiny fields. Paddocks the size of suburban lawns in the western suburbs. From which people try to scratch a living. I live on 3000 hectares, which is just big enough to lose a lot of money. Here people own, or share crop, a fraction of a hectare.

Though kilometres inland, we cross what is clearly a tidal river. Today it's drained and, on their sides, in the black ooze, lie dozens of boats. Big wooden fishing boats. Useless until the Moon waxes, commanding the waters to seek them out, to let them float again. And what's this? Australian trees. Sheoaks. Eucalypts. Did the train take a wrong turn? Suddenly we're back in Australia. Eucalypts now cover India, like weeds, and the environmental movement, such as it is, deplores them.

Landscape behaves oddly, as we slide past it, through it. In the foreground it races by. Yet the distant mountains keep pace with us, even gaining ground. It's as if the landscape was divided into slices, each positioned on a horizontal belt, each moving at different rates with, finally, one going in the wrong way. And the illusion is that the train is stationary, that it's the rest of the world that's moving.

The gumtrees have gone. Now it's palms (tall, cross-hatched trunks with detonations at the top, small green fireworks) and pylons marching over the landscape like giants made from Meccano. And clustered between them are, often as not, villages. Obviously they haven't heard of illnesses that may come from proximity to powerlines. It's as if they were seeking to derive energy from proximity. Seeking power and protection.

In India, absolutely everything looks Indian. Even the pylons. When you watch a film, you only have to see a couple of frames to know that it's set in London or Paris or Berlin. You recognise the colour of the bricks, the shape of front gates, the design of the porticoes. It's the same now. Despite the odd gum, this has to be India. The powerlines look Indian. The lamp posts look Indian. And when you pass a giant transformer, some of the wiring is so ornate that it has to be Indian. Indian baroque.

THE TRAIN

How many years is it since I've been on a train? The visual fluidity versus the bump and grind of the carriage. Oddly the feeling doesn't differ much from what you get on a 747, when you're flying through potholes at 10,000 metres. But it's more soothing on a train. The motion sedates, lulls. In the foreground bushes stampede across the screen like bison. In the middle distance, the glint of village lights. The rails mumble at the train most of the time, only shouting as it crosses a bridge. There are no other sounds in this cinema. And the contrapuntal motion is hypnotic.

The kids are still playing cricket beside the tracks, refusing to appeal against the light as the darkness moves through the air like moisture through crystals of sugar.

During the night the compartment is invaded by entire families who, ignoring our protests, clamber over us into the suspended beds. They don't have reservations. Many don't even have tickets. But they've piled on at an unscheduled stop. One by one they're evicted, responding with deafening outrage and theatrical gestures. Yet there isn't much rancour. They're replaying a familiar scene. When things calm down a conductor comes by, distributing sheets as thin as paper, blankets as cold as charity, and pillows as plump as papadams. Barricading the door against another invasion, we make our beds and lie in them.

I wake up at dawn. We're travelling north. The sun streams in through the window, or as much of it as the thick dust allows. The landscape is flat-as-a-tack but softer and lusher and beautifully, exquisitely farmed. The crops are crafted, not a blade out of place, not a head of corn or wheat allowed to be bedraggled. You'd swear everything was art directed for, yes, a movie. Any unwanted plants have been chipped or tugged. Hay has been piled into witch's hat stacks, into stacks shaped like minarets, like houses. And in the dawn, in a crimson sari, a woman is winnowing grain.

Here people are washing their clothes in the water from distant wells. Others herd the buffalo, or herd their kids to school. This at 7.30 in the morning. A solitary child, wearing only a T-shirt, stands like a soldier, ramrod stiff, watching us pass.

We are looking at thousands of years of a passivity that approaches serenity. Fate, destiny, caste, the wheel of life, reincarnation, acceptance. Versus anger, desire, ideology, revolution. And as the new century approaches there are stirrings, always stirrings. Particularly among the women who, while unwilling to speak openly as yet, are reconsidering the rules and regulations of Hinduism or rereading the Koran and beginning to dare to criticise the theology of the men.

As the sun rises the breakfast wallahs arrive. Everything is wrapped in foil. The fruit juice, its origins enigmatic, is wrapped in foil. Each of the two boiled eggs is wrapped in foil. The croissant, which is more like a mud brick, is wrapped in foil. It's as if the entire breakfast is being protected from nuclear radiation — the Bharatiya Janitor Party (the BJP) having just announced that it's going to stop pussy-footing around with nuclear policy. Perhaps the testing's already begun.

Our breakfast is brought by a large, uniformed man who doesn't smile. Indeed, if he ever smiled, at any stage in his life, he will never smile again. The various muscles that must work together to produce this pleasant expression have forgotten what to do, how to co-ordinate. Consequently the corners of the mouth now form a toppled parenthesis, as if he'd borrowed his gob from Bob Hawke. All attempts to engage him in conversation, even to thank him, are rebuffed. Is he the unhappiest man in all of India?

(Oddly enough, at the end of the journey, he will return, with a grimace that looks like a crack in a boulder. Or to maintain the prime ministerial metaphors, a grin on a granitic Malcolm Fraser. Its purpose is to elicit a tip which, when provided, is deemed inadequate. The smile instantly fades, though it lingers in the air, and the memory. The reproach of a Cheshire cat.)

It's also breakfast time on the railway station. Families are sitting in circles eating from brass bowls. A train crowded with the Indian Army slides by, their guns smothered with camouflage that doesn't work. Like the defaced advertising signs, the mesh and tarpaulins serve only to advertise.

While some people feed on the station, others are shaved on the station. Or sleep on the station. And we observe the Indian obsession for sweeping. People living in a deluge of dirt, grit and scraps of paper will sweep a tiny area with a handmade broom. A broom made of bound twigs. And no sooner have they swept than the wind will blow their efforts back to their feet. Absolutely nothing has been achieved but, nonetheless, something has been done. An attempt has been made.

Like the army's weapons, our train is camouflaged. In khaki, by dust, so that it can slip through an increasingly arid landscape without being spotted. Through a landscape now punctuated with pat-a-cake, pat-a-cake cow pats, an endless mosaic of moo-poo. For every pat is precious. They are to India what peat from the bog was to Ireland. You can burn a cow pat, getting just enough heat for cooking.

Behold mosaics of cow pats. Countless thousands of them slapped onto walls, retaining the impressions of human hands. They look like prehistoric versions of the modern hubcap, the hand as corporate logo. And like the architectural hay racks, the cow pats are piled and patted into fascinating shapes. Here a dome, there a citadel. The shapes are as inventive as the sandcastles in a competition. Come to think of it, our entire train looks as if it might have been made out of cow pats. Cow pat carriages with cow pat wheels.

Collecting cow pats is something I know about. To collect a cow pat successfully is somewhere between an art and a science. A truly desirable cow pat is round, nicely formed and free of entanglement in thick grass. It's also desirable that it contains no heavy pebbles. If a pat is too damp it will slip between the pitchfork's prongs or, worse still, between your fingers. If too dry, it will be as light as a frisbee, have the flaky consistency of a Sao biscuit, and be of little use on a garden bed. A cow pat is just right when it's been in the sun for a day or so. Then it can be safely fingered, or forked, into the barrow or the back of your ute. You want to hear a little wrenching sound as you lift it from the stubble, the tearing of a couple of strands of grass as it parts from the earth. And it's always good to have the pat reveal a couple of earthworms. The smell is not unpleasant, a bit like tobacco. And when you mound them for compost or plonk them round the rose bushes you can feel their magic, nutritional powers. Really good cow pats look rich and delicious, almost edible. And they are, of course, used as food by dung beetles. And, more mysteriously, by cattle dogs.

In India the cow pat is one of the reasons that their source, the cow, is sacred. The pat provides not only fertiliser but fuel. So the women collect them when they're just the right consistency and, shaping them in their hands, plonk them up against banks or onto brick walls where they continue to dry. Then they be ignited.

Every pat is precious. So they're treated with respect and used as a mode of artistic expression. The women form pat-a-cake, pat-a-cake patterns with them, or they mound them to resemble loaves of bread, or shape them into igloos. There are times, it seems, when the cow pat is the primary purpose of having cattle, with milk, yoghurt, cheese, ghee but by-products.

As I watch the art and architecture of the cow pat drifting by our dung-coloured, cow pat train I cannot help but notice a pungent odour. A very old lady, sitting opposite me, is farting. Farting without a hint of embarrassment. Spectacular farts are one of the memories I'll take back to Australia — including a thunderous example from a gentleman in the Lodi gardens that will wreck an interview with a famous author. I looked around for a trumpeting elephant — it could be nothing less — to discover a bloke who was subsequently identified to me as a retired policeman. He was proud rather than apologetic and gave me a beatific smile.

'Where ere you be, let your wind go free', we used to chant at school. This is a strongly held belief throughout the subcontinent.

The train comes to a grinding halt. That term, a 'grinding halt', was born on the railways, because that's what a train does. The brakes grab and grind at steel wheels which, in turn, grip at the steel tracks.

We've stopped by a blue village. The prevailing colours of villages, when they're not terracotta, are blue. But different shades of blue. You get pale blue villages, sky blue villages, fierce blue villages. Even the plastic sheets that reinforce the roofing are blue.

Behind the villages, quite often, you'll see a large building complex that has come to nothing. Immense amounts of rupees have been invested in a half-finished ghost town. Apparently projects intended to provide housing for villagers, they've run out of federal, state or development funds, or foreign aid, and are now being used as roosts for hawks. So many incomplete projects. I remember the great craters to be found in the CBDs of Sydney and Melbourne in the aftermath of the 1980s.

The train stops at Lucknow and I go for a walk. There, in the middle of the station, is an entire herd of sacred cows. Mummies, daddies, calves. But how the hell did they get here? They couldn't have jumped up from the railway tracks and it's hard to believe they climbed up and down the hundreds of stairs of the overpasses. Perhaps they were born here.

The bull makes me feel slightly homesick so I give it a scratch behind the ear. This isn't a bad bull. It's a pretty good bull. No, we're not talking a blue ribbon at the Royal Easter Show. But we're talking a big Brahman with a high hump and testicles the size of a couple of cantaloupes in a string bag. Back home you have to stuff the brutes with grass, hay or lucerne silage to get them to a decent size. Back home they can drink clean river water and breathe air so fresh that it's analogous to moral purity. But this bull lives on smog and drinks from the unimaginable muck in the gutters. And you see bulls like this eating plastic bags. Filthy ones at that. In India the cattle shamble calmly through the terrors of traffic, dodging the pedicabs, trishaws, the trucks, the dilapidated buses, the battered taxis, with absolute equanimity. And not content with surviving, they flourish. In the West, genetic engineers and artificial inseminators are trying to improve the cattle herds, and prize bulls sell for tens of thousands. But the answer in producing herds that are drought proof, fuel efficient and easy to handle may lay in cross-breeding with the herds that walk the streets, or share the railway platforms with the commuters.

Until recently I had a huge Brahman bull, built like a brick dunny, that I called Malcolm X, in honour of his darkness and dignity. We were looking at a yardful of bulls, trying to choose one, when Malcolm chose me. He pushed his way through the others and touched me with his tongue. It wasn't a lick. It was a taste, tentative and delicate. With the tip of his tongue. Now, Brahman bulls aren't meant to behave that way but he kept behaving oddly. I could call him across a 100-hectare paddock and he'd come trotting like a puppy dog. If I found him lying in the grass I could sit on him. If I walked towards him he'd lower his massive head and, despite my own considerable bulk, lift me into the air, in a slow-motion variation of what a bull might do savagely to a bullfighter in the ring. We were great pals, Malcolm X and I. But he had a bad habit of walking through fences, electric or barbed wire, when he went on strolls. He'd have 100 metres of fence trailing behind him, like a wedding train, as he sought female companionship. And Patrice and the farm manager thought he was a very dangerous bull, that he'd finish up killing me. So one day, when I was in Sydney, slaving over a hot microphone, they sold him. My sacred bull.

What a train ticket buys you in India are endless squabbles. You can queue at railway stations for days on end, have prolonged and acrimonious negotiations with station managers and cop misinformation about availabilities and timetables. But even then the bureaucracy hasn't done with you. Which is why there are three ticket collectors on the train. One man checks the ticket. If you've neglected to buy one prior to climbing on board, the second collector collects your money. And the third collector — actually he's a filler — fills out the forms. The trio are at the tail end of dozens of people who are employed to provide you with ticketing in a long and continuously broken line of communication. A line of communication that's like the wires and fence posts tugged from their place by Malcolm X. Thinking back it took the best efforts of five travel agents, including the in-house bloke at the High Commission, to get us on this train. And it has taken all our efforts, and arguments, to stay on it.

We begin to move again, the platform sliding away. And the next session in the endless cinema of Indian life begins with, as usual, a screening of the hand-painted Val Morgan signs. Where the Reeboks look like cars, and the cars like Reeboks.

2

Mumbai

The biggest paddock in Australia is the long paddock. Not even the Vesty boys or Kidman could command the same acreage. It's the space between the barbed wire fence and the road where cattle feed when the drought is bad. Come the tough times and you'll see the drovers working those endless stretches, trying to keep their herds alive.

In Mumbai the main roads are the long bedroom. Between the airport and the city countless people are living hard, sprawled out on a dirty sheet or lying neatly on a scrap of blanket, head pillowed by a couple of rags.

In Australia we put out our dustbins at night. In Mumbai, people put themselves out, as if they were rubbish waiting to be collected. There are figures lying everywhere but, around midnight, the population is densest under the street lamps.

Why there? Do they feel safe? Does their visibility make them feel less afraid? Wouldn't the pool of light attract more insects? Perhaps it's because the light serves to define an area, to create a sense of territory. The light turns its little bit of the street into a room; a room where the walls are made of blackness.

The light pushes back the darkness but not the noise. The racket is deafening. How can people possibly sleep? They're inches away from the endless jam of Mumbai traffic, from the deep beat of heavy trucks. But perhaps the blanketing fug of diesel that pours from a thousand exhausts helps to heat the room created by the street light.

The numbers thin out in the CBD and in the better suburbs. But you find the sleeping figures again, around the next corner. I remember the Entombed Warriors in Xian — the endless ranks of terracotta statues silent and erect — with hundreds more awaiting release from the black earth. In Mumbai the ranks of the sleeping are just as awesome and surprising.

In Xian, the figures stand. You see their faces. In Mumbai, they're prone. You see the backs of their heads because most sleep face down. Here is a mother in a sari. On one side, her little boy, perhaps three. On the other, her little girl, perhaps four. The three of them, still as terracottas. The weather is pleasant this evening, neither too hot nor too cold. But what happens in the rain? What happens in the long monsoon? Oh God, what happens in the rain?

Oh God, oh gods. Here in a country of so many gods, of Hindu gods beyond count, of Christian and Muslim gods, of Sikh and Jain and Zoroastrian gods. On this plinth a statue of Nehru. Nearby a statue of the Mahatma. Nehru symbolises secular humanism, Gandhi passionate ecumenicalism. Is there not enough holiness, enough humanism, to deal with this problem?

There are many pornographies, of which the best known is far and away the least harmful. Sexual pornography comes a bad last to the pornographies of violence, of patriotism, of war. But the worst of the porns, and the first of them, the most obscene of them, is the pornography of poverty.

It's not the naked limbs of the sexual gymnasts in the amateurishly made movies that represent the depth of depravity. It's the skeletal limbs of these thousands upon thousands of homeless people. Why waste moral outrage on silicon breasts? Look at the bloated stomachs of malnourished children.

The pornographies of sex and violence are produced by taboos — by the lies and the obfuscations surrounding sex and death. But the pornography of poverty isn't subject to a taboo. This pornography has always been encouraged by those on high. You can recruit your cheap labour from the poor and the powerless, not to mention your soldiers. That's been true throughout history. It was a truth renewed in the Vietnam War where, despite the perjured evidence of movies starring John Wayne or Tom Cruise, it was young black men, from the ghettos, too powerless to elude the call-up, who were most heavily represented at the front line and in the body bags.

And it's certainly true in India where the poor exist to make the rich feel richer. Even though the well-to-do may tut-tut over the 300 million of their fellow citizens who are acknowledged to be poverty-stricken.

'Stricken' is a good word. The poor are strickened with disease, with ignorance and despair. But they do not give up without a fight. It's hard to see evidence of that fight at a political level — not much sign of the poor becoming militant and engaging in significant and effective political struggles. But they fight, as best they can, for their children, their lives and their scraps of dignity. And you cannot help but be impressed by the poor of India, humbled by their vitality, their determination, even by their humour.

It's very late at night and the stuffiness of the hotel and the meaningless racket of the useless air-conditioner make sleep impossible. The television gives me a choice of an Indian movie — wherein yet another Brylcreem'd piece of beefcake pursues another giggling virgin through some more papier-mâché trees — and yet another lot of hyperventilated reporters from CNN. So I grope my way down the dark stairs and head for the main shopping drag where, just hours ago, hundreds of thousands of people were squeezed between the shops and the wooden display stands that stall owners use for their stocks of sunglasses, belts, audio cassettes, scarves, brass elephants and smuggled cigarettes.

The long paddock. The long bedroom. The long arcade. If there's a piece of footpath that hasn't been dug up — to fix the drains or lay some telephone cables — it's immediately occupied by a family selling milk from their cow or a bloke squeezing oranges into chipped glasses.

But the milk vendor has taken his cow home, and the stands are empty, shrouded in sheets of dirty canvas, and you tread warily to avoid the jagged-edged pits, the asphalt upheavals and the unconscious. Let sleeping dogs lie, and they do, oblivious of the cats which, in turn, ignore the rats scurrying past, and over, the sleeping figures. The cats are wise to look away — the rats are big and healthy, the cats anorexic.

If the sleepers don't have some rags to soften the footpath, they'll use a sheet of black plastic or a flattened cardboard box. Some sleep neatly, their bodies pressed out of the way, up against the shopfronts, but others have abandoned themselves across my path. Their faces twitch in their sleep, their mouths move in their dreams. One figure catches my attention because what seems to be his only possession in the world is placed so precisely beside him on his flattened box. A plastic toothbrush down to its final bristles.

I find two young men who are still awake, playing cards on a foul-smelling step. Hands blur in the shuffling. The dealing is rat-a-tat-tat rapid. The bets are tersely whispered.

Let sleeping dogs lie. And they lie everywhere, large, yellow and dingo-like. They don't seem to belong to anyone in particular. They're not sleeping in alignment with their loyalties. Their faces, too, twitch. And some are whimpering in their dreams.

It's 2 am on Mumbai's busiest shopping street. The majority sleeping here are men, lonely men. And lonely dogs. The homeless families prefer the wider footpaths along the airport road. A herd of goats trots by. Figures emerge from the darkest of the darkness, from the foulest of the doorways, whispering temptations. Drugs? I shake my head. Girls? Then boys? Okay, what about change your money? I find the best way to deal with them is to turn suddenly and to snarl: 'Fuck off!'

Apart from porters squabbling over luggage, or drivers arguing over a collision, raised voices are rare here. So, 'Fuck off' resonates, particularly in the long bedroom.

Next morning the world of commerce clocks on and the nightshift is vanished, banished. Or perhaps the sleepers have just dusted themselves down and become the stall holders. Is even the shabbiest of them a hustler, a businessman, an entrepreneur?

I push through the crowds to Leopold's restaurant, complete with its crudely painted mural of tourist icons: the Eiffel Tower, the Statue of Liberty, the Pyramids, the House of Commons, St

Basil's in Red Square and, yes, Sydney's Opera House. Indian painters have yet to work out the laws of perspective. When they attempt it they, like the painters of ancient Rome, get it arse about so that the foreground recedes while the background advances. Esher would enjoy the Leopold's murals, just as the tourists and the counter-culture pilgrims are enjoying the Leopold's great dollops of cheap food. Since getting a glowing reference in *Lonely Planet*, the Michelin Guide for backpackers, the place is full of born-again hippies. The 1960s are alive and well and living in Leopold's.

It wasn't so long ago that the beats and the beatniks, the *dharma* bums seeking religious ecstasy in drugs, the kids from California chanting *Hare Krishna* determined to change their names to something more polychromatic, intent on checking on every *maharishi* and entering every *ashram*, arrived in India in their millions. (Remember when India's official airline ran an ad offering 'Nirvana for $100 a day'?) The gurus didn't help them to acquire the tranquillity that comes, in Indian writer Gita Mehta's words, 'from the oriental ability to see in a plethora of contradictions a literally mind-blowing affirmation'. She was right; to go from the monomania of the West to the multimania of the East was as painful a business as a sex change. And the flies and the dysentery didn't help.

Now the pilgrims have given up chanting mantras in favour of therapy or Prozac. Yet you still see kids, including middle-aged kids, trying to locate, and follow, the old hippie trail. 'Trying a little hash, a little meditation,' says Mehta, 'a little astrology, a little Buddhism. A lot of sex.'

Sardus and gurus still abound, fighting for their share in a decreasing market. And people from the culture of instant gratification still persist in seeking instant spirituality. Books on holy subjects — yoga, *tantra*, the *gita*, the *Upanishads* — still crowd the shelves of the bookshops in the hotel foyers.

The export market for gurus is down these days, though the *maharishis'* Transcendental Meditation (copyright, patent pending) still recruits people who want to fly without an airline ticket. But the bounce seems to be out of the Hare Krishna who, these days, are rarely seen doing their spiritual conga-line through the shopping malls. When their guru died the internecine squabbling got very nasty indeed, as members of the hierarchy murdered each other. And the Orange People did themselves in at the same time. Gone are their immense communes of acolytes and the vast warehouses full of Rolls Royces. Fortunately, the Ananda Marga have ceased their bombings and no longer demand self-immolation from young female devotees, particularly those with access to a parental bank account.

'Krishna still rolls his pat of butter, Devi still sits cross-legged and bare-breasted on a lotus, and Ganesh, hip thrust out, smiles his elephant smile,' says Mehta, 'but karma isn't what it used to be.'

Of course, karma doesn't proffer a heaven. Only a great many lives. It doesn't proffer an afterlife. The final achievement is death.

Though the poorest of tourists, they're rich beyond the dreams of avarice to the beggars who walk and stalk the streets. There's the blind Muslim with his white cap and tunic, his white stick, his white eyes. The village woman beating a tiny drum — and beating it well — while her two-year-old child darts among the restaurant tables, avoiding the blows of the waiters. And suddenly there's a stick insect — no, a daddy long legs — a human trunk held high from the ground on four of the frailest imaginable appendages. Four legs, of which two might once have been arms. He/she moves quickly, scuttling among the legs of the shoppers.

Begging is strident, assertive, desperate. And you give because it's a judgment on you, not on the beggar. You give in guilt and anger and disgust and weariness. Or you don't give. And most don't. They are blind to the faces, deaf to the voices.

And you wonder whether the beggars take credit cards in the financial district. No, you don't wonder that at all. But it's one of the jokes that people make to protect themselves from the all-pervasive horrors.

In Varanasi begging is a ritual. In Mumbai it's a transaction. Everything is buying and selling. In prostitution, in high finance, in the provision of labour. The transaction in beggary? It involves shame, pity, revulsion and guilt. In each transaction you buy a few moments of self-justification.

I'm confronted by a boy with one arm, from which the hand

seems to have been burnt, or melted. He extends his stump in plea. I produce a torn 10 *rupee* bill, but what am I supposed to do with it? Shove it in his mouth as if that were a letterbox? He gestures with the stump. I'm to tuck it into a fold of cloth, a sort of marsupial pouch for money, between his abbreviated arm and his collar. As I do so, I can feel the warmth of his body, the beat of his heart. There are already a few coins in the pouch. He's thrilled with the note and gives me a dazzling smile. He has an imperfect body but perfect teeth.

Later, I'm haggling over a taxi fare. I'm being ripped off, just as I have been virtually every time I've climbed into a vehicle, whether it had two, three or four wheels. The bill has been doubled, redoubled. But we're talking three or four dollars, for Christ sake! Pay the bloke! Fill his hands with these valueless coins! And think yourself lucky that you're not him, the taxi driver. And give extra to beggars, and think yourself lucky that you're not the amputee, the leper, the freak, the horror whose body is like a triumph of prosthetic make-up for a Halloween movie.

But in the seconds that your eyes meet, if you cannot avoid that second, and God knows how hard you try to avoid it, you see yourself. You see your entirely undeserved, random-chance good fortune. You see your problems, personal, professional, financial, in the proper perspective. And you feel ashamed for your health, wealth and privilege. And you feel the fear of mortality — for there's death in the deformity of leprosy, in the amputations of an agricultural or industrial accident, in the implacable progress of disease. In paying a few cents, you're buying time, abbreviating Purgatory.

There is a roar of sound. I look up and see a local train in the sky; a train where all the seats and standing room are taken, from which people dangle like bunches of grapes. My heart stops as I wait for someone to fall, to lose a limb or two, and thus be recruited to the ranks of beggars.

The so-called Gateway to India, the over-engineered piece of nonsense that combines the Indian fortress with the Roman triumphal arch, an uneasy hybrid that might have been designed by one of Josef Stalin's architects, was built to greet a British royal whose identity almost every citizen of Mumbai disputes. Was it Victoria? Edward? One of the Georges? Whatever, whoever, it's now seen as a symbol of Indian independence but serves as the location of some of the most frenzied begging in town.

There I met Bob. That's what the boy calls himself. Bob is a vivacious nine year old with a dazzling smile, dancing eyes and an ability to look every which way at once; all the better to keep an eye on the cops and on the competing kids, or to spot better prospects than yourself for the *baksheesh*.

Bob tells me that he comes in every morning on the train and goes home when it's dark, hopefully with enough money to help buy 'powdered milk for his baby sister'. Later I realise that all the kids talk of 'powdered milk for my sister'. It is the code for *baksheesh*, turning base metal or torn currency into the gold of charity. By buying powdered milk for his baby sister Bob isn't begging. Or if he is, he's not begging for himself.

Bob started with the usual international question, the simple, tactical question that you're asked in Cairo, in Denpasar, in the favelas of Rio. The question that, if you answer it, has you engaged. 'Where are you from?' If you don't answer the questioner will persist. 'Are you America? England? Germany?' If you admit to being anything, Australian for example, your interrogator will register astonishment and pleasure. How amazing to be England, Germany, Australia. Almost as amazing as being America.

Bob pops the questions and I answer. Now we are friends. Bob has a dialogue going. And he attaches himself to me like a limpet. Which I accept because he'll help me ward off the advances of others. In an instant he's not just a beggar but he's *my* beggar, and halfway to being my bodyguard.

I find myself asking questions of Bob that he answered as best he can in his jumbled vocabulary.

Why isn't he at school? When did he stop going? Doesn't that worry him? Do the strolling police hit him with their bamboo poles? Does he really have a sister? What of his father?

Finally I agree to help him buy powdered milk and he pockets the money with pleasure. Then he scampers off, giving one of the dozens of dogs that hang around, begging from the beggars, a kick up its arse. Not an unkind kick. More of a triumphant one. With kids like Bob it's not the end of the world if you don't give him anything. They'll tap dance around a little and circle back and find another target. 'Who are you? Australia? America? England? Germany?'

Poverty is grinding. It grinds away at the human spirit like train wheels grind rails. But for a while you'll see a shower of sparks — in the cheek and defiance of a kid like Bob. There's something heroic about the boy you won't find in the best and brightest at Mumbai's finest private schools. What a pity that for all his charm and spontaneity he hasn't got a future.

Most parents would be proud of a kid like Bob. Proud of his self-reliance, his shrewdness and optimism. However, Bob will age quickly. His life expectancy isn't great. Among the poor in India, even the rural poor, it rarely is. A friend who spent a lifetime studying village life, tells me that he rarely sees anyone in those rural communities over the age of fifty. And if he does see someone who's fifty, he or she will look like they're eighty. He shows me some of the photographs he's prepared for an exhibition which he hopes will ignite Indian public opinion. I see the faces of octogenarians born in the 1950s.

Poverty gives business people their tiffin-wallahs. It gives them servants who'll clean, scour, cook and shop and babysit. It provides chauffeurs who'll keep a high polish on their new Mercedes. Trouble is the destitute lower property values with their humpies, or when they lie like bundles of rags on bundles of rags on the footpath. So the burghers of Mumbai had their shanties pushed down and pushed many of them out of town. Now they have to catch the trains back in — long journeys in suffocating conditions, in trains so crowded that when people die in them nobody notices until the carriage empties out and the corpse collapses to the floor. Carriages so crowded that, its said, people can have sexual intercourse while standing without their neighbours noticing.

Mumbai is home to the largest slum in Asia, the dark heart of a wealthy city and home to about 700,000 people. Yet from this ghastly place come some of India's most beautiful artifacts — silver and gold embroidery, jewellery, pottery, cloth and leather goods which fetch high prices in the tourist and international markets. This is the richest city in India, providing a third of the tax revenue to the Indian Government.

No Australian has any right to criticise Mumbai. As a child

I read *Oliver Twist* with disbelief — the horror stories of Dickens' gutter snipes, of Fagin's pocket pickers. And I read Hugo's accounts of the Paris underworld. It was reassuring to know that I was reading of the distant past, that we'd never see such days again. So when I thought about India it was with a feeling of superiority, of condescension. Imagine a country where people sleep on footpaths! Where Brahmins step over the dying and the dead.

Forty years on we've introduced the worlds of Hugo and Dickens to the cities of Australia. It is possible to go along to a production of *Les Mis*, to feel stirred by the music and libretto, and then to push your way through the street kids as you return to your car, to avert your eyes from the people who live on the footpaths and under railway bridges. The people who fight for the right to sleep in a charity bin. The numbers of homeless people in Australia are a tiny fraction of India's but, as a percentage of the population, we're doing pretty well.

A torso with arms skates around me on his billycart, holding things that look like irons in his calloused hands, to give them some protection from the roads. Is it only a matter of time until I see the lower part of a body running around? A body without a torso? With nothing from the waist up? You can't help but make bad jokes about beggars because of the horror of it. The horror and the energy. For the beggars are exuberant, proactive.

Many of the beggars here, and in Calcutta, are dispossessed small farmers — forced to the city where they suffer more dispossession, descending from the ranks of the unemployed to beggary. Here they live in homes made from rubbish that, all too often, will be burnt or bulldozed by the authorities. Here they are reduced to eating, literally, the scraps from the rich man's table, and sharing them with the rats. Yet they maintain a spirit. You see it in the street kids who dance and prance beside you, in the kids like Bob by the Gateway of India. Dickens' artful dodgers, artfully dodging the traffic and the blows of passers-by, maintaining an audacity, an insouciance, that provokes and charms.

When darkness falls I wander along a causeway towards a mosque that seems to be floating in the harbour. Every step of the way there are people selling costume jewellery, plastic toys, sundry kitsch. They pump furiously at their hurricane lamps, so that you can see exactly what they're selling. But as you get closer to the luminosity of the mosque, as white, as tiled and curved as Utzon's Opera House, the beggars take over — and they're selling pity, guilt, horror and tradition. Many have children like rag dolls, some extend hands, others stumps. But the most effective and profitable begging is also the most spectacular. It comes from a chorus line, a floorshow. Half a dozen lepers (I presume they were lepers but they might have been multiple amputees or victims of foetal abnormality) have formed a pattern on the ground, a sort of star shape. And they writhe and kick their abbreviated legs. This is Busby Berkeley begging — reminiscent of one of those vast set-ups where Mr Berkeley put his dancers on the floor and his camera on the roof. And to accompany their bizarre cavortings they sing a song, in a compelling, edgy harmony. Not only do they get most of the money from the throngs heading for the mosque, but they deserve it, both for the degree of their disability and for the originality of their presentation. It isn't enough to donate. I feel like clapping them as well.

At the end of the road, just before the marble stairs that lead to the mosque, there's a long row of more conventional beggars with one or two coins in their bowls or on the asphalt before them. And finally I come upon a woman counting coins; piles of small coins of rice-grain denomination. So are the beggars members of a collective? Do the less confronting beggars join forces in this way, so as to compete with the Busby Berkeley floorshow? Do they average out the take, dividing the spoils so that each one can be sure of at least getting something? If so, the lepers remained an independent act.

The poor are always with us, most of all in Mumbai. The next day, trying to find a famous bookshop, I am surrounded by young mothers, or maybe older sisters, clutching babies to flat breasts. Children perhaps twelve months old who, already, know how to tug at a sleeve — and the heart — how to smile, how to look pitiful. They are double-acts, these babies and young women. And you learn that if you give money you should not expect to be thanked. Not that you seek thanks so much as expiation. You give for release, for relief. You pay the beggars as a form of toll. Otherwise you have no right of passage. You discover that to give money is to up the ante. A small donation simply isn't good enough, while a larger one displays weakness and vulnerability and means that the demands will escalate; that you'll be treated as a desperately needed resource.

Other beggars will come, appearing out of nowhere, with other mothers or big sisters with one-year-old children. And there'll be a chorus of clamouring as upturned palms, big and little, are thrust eagerly into your face, like bouquets of carnivorous flowers.

What I most vividly remember are the babies, each of whom was a joy to behold. For all their filth and rags they are beautiful, beautiful kids. As imbued with life and intelligence and entitlement as the kids of the wealthiest white Australians in South Yarra or Bellevue Hill.

This is one of the few places on Earth where the Australian dollar counts. It counts for 25 *rupees*. Most things are cheap when you divide them into quarters. But into 25ths? Mumbai is your opportunity to eat well, to order another glass (dulled by a million scratches) brimming with orange or mango or pineapple juice. Here's an opportunity to give people some money, to spread it around a little. But it's also a society where everyone expects to haggle. Even the beggars haggle. So if you give insufficiently, at least to the professional beggars working the strip, it may be returned to you with the not entirely amiable suggestion that you double it.

Everyone everywhere is haggling. Some of them are Australian. How is it you can always pick an accent across a crowded cafe, or across a crowded crowd, when you can't begin to decipher the words? You only have to hear a hint, a nasality, a timbre to know that the person is Australian or French or American. And everywhere, in every accent, people are arguing with taxi drivers, stall holders, railway porters and waiters over 50 *rupees* here or there. Tourists haggle as a matter of pride, trying to give half of what they've asked for and a tenth of what is deserved when, in fact, they're dealing with a few cents. Yet most of us will spend ten minutes arguing over 50 *rupees*. Two dollars for an Australian. One for an American.

The contrasts in Mumbai are heightened when I'm taken to

an expensive Bengali restaurant where we see that flesh, rather than bones, is fashionable. The people here, Mumbai's business class, are huge. So much so that 'stark contrast' is inappropriate when you compare them to the tiny people who crowd the streets and, most of all, to the bird-like beggars. How can you account for the immensity of the rich? Is it a consequence of being better fed for generations? Or is it something that has happened quickly, explosively, like the boom in Mumbai's economy?

Throughout India you see attempts to hybridise foreign influence, but this restaurant is pure jet set, cloned from London or New York. The paintings are Saatchi and Saatchi, the glass sculptures from a gallery in Tribeca. Yet the food, served in vast amounts, to the vast patrons, is defiantly regional.

In the West the wealthy live by the aphorism of the late Duchess of Windsor: 'You can't be too rich or too thin'. In India, no one wants to be thin, least of all the rich, who seem intent on weighing themselves in jewellery, particularly gold chains. They are Gullivers in Lilliput, and if the boom in India's economy continues, the rich of India will block the sun from the poor who, while remaining innumerable, will take up less and less space and political concern.

The people I pity most in India are the trishaw and rickshaw drivers, the little blokes with skeletal legs who have to press their bare feet onto the metal pedals, heaving with all their might so that they can shift, three, four times their weight in human cargo or in freight, or both. Once they get the bike moving, the laws of physics are on their side. But the traffic stops them after a couple of pedals. So the immense heaving begins again. Behind them, riding high, might be an over-upholstered couple, his belly bulging over his belt, her folds of flesh spilling from her sari. And there he is, this human horse, this pit pony, straining and frowning as he attempts to extract another ounce of effort from his undernourished, underweight body.

No wonder you see them lying around deeply asleep. They seem to fall asleep as soon as they unload their passengers. They are the cheapest form of transport, but they pay a heavy price for their profession.

Then comes the modified motor scooters — metal carapaces stuck on the back of Vespas and Lambrettas. The screaming two-strokes can barely pull their load. You feel almost as sorry for the engines as you do for the cyclists. The trishaw will cost you a couple of *rupees* for a lengthy trip. You'll pay double for a two-stroke engine — and double again for an ancient taxi.

There are even cheaper rides than the trishaw provides. There's also the rickshaw, where bare feet pound the shattered asphalt, where members of the schedule castes drag their betters through the crowded streets. I'd rather crawl over broken glass than ride in one. And, yet, in saying that, in feeling that, I'm denying the rickshaw driver a few extra *rupees* he desperately needs. The rickshaws are like scales of injustice with the load outweighing the bloke between the shafts.

Like many Western cities, Mumbai is de-industrialising. This is likely to displace many of the five or six million traditionally employed in the industrial and self-employed sector. 'But we won't need to kick anyone out,' says the secretary of the Bombay Chamber of Commerce and Industry, 'market forces will automatically do that.' Along with pollution, congestion, and the high price of land.

3

Gandhi

'What do I think of Western civilisation?' said Gandhi. 'I think it would be a good idea.'

Mohandas Karamchand, later to be known as the Mahatma, was born in 1869 and, responding indifferently to an indifferent education, went on to practise Law in London where he came into contact with George Bernard Shaw and the Fabians. During this era he was a dapper little bloke, wearing spats and a bowler hat, carrying a furled umbrella and taking violin lessons.

Returning to India his legal practice in Bombay was highly successful, providing him with an income of 5000 pounds a year — but he gave it up in 1893 to live on a quid a week in South Africa where he spent the next 21 years fighting white bigotry. Not bigotry against Africans. Bigotry against Indians, expressed in abuse, verbal and physical, and discriminatory legislation.

Ghandi's experiences in South Africa not only politicised him but radicalised him. He returned to India in 1914 and though supporting the British in the First World War, became involved in Swaraj, the Home Rule Movement, becoming the driving force in the Congress Organisation.

Gandhi's role in Civil Disobedience earned him jail sentences for conspiracy — he was imprisoned from 1922 to 1924. A few years later he led his long march to the sea, to collect salt in symbolic defiance of the government monopoly. In a campaign without press secretaries, spin doctors or CNN, with only the telegraph wire to alert the villages in his path, his lonely trek became an immense protest. By the time he reached the ocean Gandhi led an army of thousands. He had created a mass movement.

(Seventy years on, Northern India has all but run out of salt. Salt traders are hoarding, forcing prices up, and panic buying has led to salt disappearing from shops. In Patna the price of salt has increased tenfold. Across the nation Indians are spending almost 40 per cent more on food than they were a year ago. It seems that India will end the century with one of its greatest crises, with millions more joining the ranks of the desperately poor.)

Gandhi was reimprisoned and, on his release the following year, negotiated a truce between the government and Congress, attending the London round-table conference on Indian constitutional reform. On his return to India he was promptly arrested; a pattern that would be repeated over and over again.

At the outbreak of war, Gandhi argued that only a free India could give Britain effective support — so he urged complete independence as a matter of urgency. He was then accused of obstructing the war effort and another arrest followed.

Gandhi lived to see India granted independence, describing it as 'the noblest act of the British nation'. But he was heartbroken by the cruelties and butcheries that marked Partition, which would have been even worse had he not begun his 'fast to the death' to shame the ethnic cleansers. Then, on 30 January 1948, ten days after a previous attempt on his life, he was assassinated, in a garden, on his way to a prayer meeting, by a Hindu fanatic, a member of a hard-line organisation associated with the new BJP government.

'The great soul' was greatly loved. Yet many saw him as megalomaniacal, as someone held in the thrall of self-delusion. He was particularly disinclined to face the violence that his 'non-violent' campaigns evoked. Gandhi's achievements as a pacifist, as the architect of passive resistance, were only possible because of the violence of others.

On the day before he died, Gandhi said: 'Even if I die in the service of this nation, I would be proud of it. Every drop of my blood I'm sure would contribute to the growth of this nation and make it strong and dynamic.' These are unashamedly messianic words, not so much 'I have a dream' as 'I am the dream'. Either way, it was a pretty good dream. 'Non-violence is the first article of my faith,' he'd say, 'it is also the last article of my creed.' One can imagine how he'd have felt as India gatecrashed the nuclear club and sent South Asia spiralling into the immense expense and incalculable dangers of an arms race.

Gandhi was Lord of the Luddites. He wanted to smash the deafening machines of cloth production. For him the old spinning wheel was as important as the prayer wheel to the monks in Lhasa. 'I claim that in losing the spinning wheel we lost our left lung. We are, therefore, suffering from galloping consumption. The restoration of the wheel arrests the progress of the disease.'

Decades later, Gandhi lingers on. You see him on the bank notes. On flower-garlanded photographs dangling from the stalls of hawkers. He's become a dark-skinned version of St Christopher, swinging from the rear vision mirrors of taxis. Everywhere you see pictures of the little man with big ears and a big smile, looking like an intelligent Bill McMahon.

The last footsteps the Mahatma took are marked in blood-red concrete, in crude bas-reliefs of his bare feet. The footsteps look funny at first, like something out of a Warner Bros cartoon. Or like the fossilised tracks of a long dead creature. Which is, after all, exactly what they are.

Little bandy Gandhi, the man described by Winston Churchill as 'that half-naked fakir' lived in a bungalow in Delhi and died in the garden. The concrete footsteps leave the little room where he slept and ate a final meal, and cross a small courtyard before moving along a long, straight path.

I'm fascinated by them. They're both poignant and comical. But are they accurate? Are we to believe that Gandhi had an amanuensis who marked his every footfall? Is it possible that left and right have been transposed? Or that his progress was less purposeful, more meandering?

A couple of kids appear, a little girl about nine and a younger brother. They delight in the footsteps, playing a form of hopscotch on them, small bare feet following the saint's progress.

The Indian Christ, Gandhi is the Messiah who had to die. Those who chose to follow his example in other cultures had an equally poor prognosis. Martin Luther King, America's great Gandhian, lived with the fear of assassination until, finally, the bullets found him. It was an assassination that would kill not only the man but the dream, handing over African-American leadership to the militant Malcolm X and, in due course, to the Muslim zealot Louis Farrakhan. And death was the final accolade paid to the pop cultural Gandhi, John Lennon, who'd learnt from an Indian guru that 'all you need is love'. Having astonished himself with the discovery that he was more famous than Jesus Christ, Lennon too would be executed.

Mandela? He was never a Gandhian. His secular sainthood was achieved as the head of an organisation that never shied from violence. His beatification was a consequence of his transcending that violence, and of the awful fact that the ANC was less brutal than apartheid's security forces.

I look up at an enormous statue of Gandhi and wonder what the poor old bloke would have made of the India at his bronzed feet. And I wonder what, if anything, he means to a new generation of the upwardly mobile with their cellular phones?

His image is one of the most reproduced, replicated and revered in all of human history — up there with Rameses, Mao Tse-tung, Napoleon, St Joan and the Virgin Mary. Not even the cult of Lenin's personality, in the halcyon days of the Soviet Union, produced more effigies.

The Mahatma is, of course, far more worthy of sculptural attention than Vladimir Ilyich. And at least his embalmed corpse isn't a tourist attraction, like Lenin's or Mao's. Yet the endless repetitions of his image, and the commercialism that surrounds it, represent an immense devaluation of the currency and would have disgusted the man himself.

There's a fast-fading fresco of Gandhi's life beside the place where he was gunned down — a comic book minus the talk balloons. It is designed to tell his story to the multitude of visitors of whom many, if not most, are unable to read. And it does so with commendable candour, eschewing the hagiography of the pamphlets for sale at the kiosk. For example, it reminds us that the imagery of Gandhi, the iconographic, trademark of the Mahatma, was as calculated, as art-directed as any exercise in corporate or imperial history.

As the fresco reminds us, Gandhi's redesign, his corporate workover was every bit as deliberate. The Christ of India is depicted as an anglophile lawyer in London. Then, after his humiliations in Johannesburg, you see him sitting down in front of a small mirror and hacking off his hair. Then the reinvented Gandhi emerges as the bald, half-naked fakir — the transformation from the dapper to the *dhoti* as astonishing as Clark Kent's metamorphosis into Superman. Which, come to think of it, isn't an entirely inappropriate analogy.

Looking at the fresco, as abundant with detail as a dozen Breughels, I remember the movie of Gandhi which, in turn, takes me back to the Great Wall of China. It's just before the Tiananmen Square massacres and I'm on a cultural delegation with the likes of David Williamson, Noni Hazlehurst and Jack Thompson with stereophonic girlfriends. We've climbed a steep section of the wall, the one usually used for photo opportunities, when we see a tubby little bloke heading our way. He's perspiring even more than we are. It's one of the Attenborough brothers, the one who makes blockbuster movies as opposed to the one who climbs into termites' nests. Among his epics were the clunkers *A Bridge Too Far* (known in the trade as *A Film Too Long*) and *Chaplin*, the film that succeeded in convincing a modern audience that Charles was a boring fart rather than one of the greatest artists since Leonardo. And a damned sight funnier.

We argue over his praenomen as he approaches and agree that this Attenborough is Richard. Indeed, Sir Richard. And we ask him what he's doing in China. 'I'm here trying to sell *Gandhi*.'

'I'm going very well,' he insists, 'I've shown *Gandhi* to all the senior party officials.'

So what? Senior party officials see all the movies. Madame Mao spent half her life in a private cinema watching pirated prints of all the films she'd never allow the multitudes to see. And it was just the same in Moscow.

'But Gandhi? What's offensive about Gandhi?' asks Attenborough. 'He was a pacifist.'

Exactly, a pacifist. And the Chinese despise pacifism.

Years later, the Chinese allow a Gandhian film to be released — *E.T.* — starring a little bloke with the same big eyes, the same big ears, a dark-skinned body. Another half-naked fakir. But by then they were in an advanced state of ideological confusion.

I cross the city to the Raj Ghat where, the day after his murder, Gandhi's body was cremated. The tourist buses are parked bumper-to-bumper, with nook and cranny occupied by ice-cream salesmen or a nut vendor. An old woman sits at the gates, the orange of her sari blending with the colour of the flowers she sells to the tourists and the pilgrims. A sign, haphazardly lettered and gloriously misspelt, urges people to be respectful — not to play games or eat or drink on the lawns. Yet the greatest disrespect to the place comes from the official Mahatma gift shop that sells hagiographies of the Mahatma in every known language, along with Mahatma kitsch and badly dubbed cassettes of 'The Mahatma's Favourite Music'. These songs, mainly popular ones, are played so loudly that the high notes have shredded the speaker cones. The cacophony makes it impossible to approach the shop — you bounce back from the wall of sound. And they probably wonder why they rarely sell anything.

On the Raj Ghat there are monuments to others with the same name — Indira and Rajiv. Others that came to the same end. Like that other great democracy, the USA, India is a country where the course of history is regularly changed by a bullet.

Though it may seem the most mixed of metaphors, every messiah signs a Mephistophelean contract. The job is self-sacrificial, with martyrdom essential to myth. Thus martyrs abound in the United States, from the political to the pop cultural, from Lincoln to Lennon. Certainly it has become an Indian tradition to assassinate Gandhis, even if their connection to him was through the family business of Congress rather than family. Indira would be assassinated in 1984 by her Sikh bodyguard resentful of her employment of troops to storm the Golden Temple at Amritsar. And Rajiv, the older son of Indira and grandson of Nehru, would die at the hands, and other body parts, of a Tamil suicide bomber.

Are they still assassinating the Mahatma? I talked to Gita Mehta, author of *Karma Cola* and *Snakes and Ladders*, about Gandhi. Hasn't he been made into a god and, therefore, made remote and irrelevant?

'More than a god,' says Gita, 'he's often been made an

excuse. You know, for years David Lean wanted to film his story and was always told, "If you ever make a film of Gandhi, do not make him into a god. He was too great a man."

'My theory has always been that, of the four great players of the subcontinent — Mountbatten, Nehru, Jinnah and Gandhi — three were anglicised. Gandhi was the only one who had the arrogance (and to me it was arrogance: Gandhi's humility came out of a fantastic sense of assurance which is essentially arrogant) to wear a loincloth into the very heart of the British Empire.

'Churchill thundered in Parliament: "This nauseating spectacle of a seditious lawyer turned half-naked fakir mounting the steps of the Viceroy's house to parlay on equal terms with the representative of the King Emperor of India." It was the nakedness, it was the parlaying, it was the horror that he was climbing up the steps of imperial power. And when the Viceroy said to him, "Will you have some sugar in your tea?" he said, "No, I prefer a pinch of salt." Because salt was so symbolic. And he made a point of speaking to all the menial staff in the Viceroy's house. He sat and ate curry with the Indians in the Viceroy's kitchens. He was the ultimate threat.

'Gandhi was the savviest politician India has ever known. And it was savvy to go to London in a loincloth.'

4

The Untouchables

I followed Gandhi's footsteps as far as I could. They led along a yellow brick road that wound its way up the highest hill in Delhi to the mighty palace of a powerful man. Who turned out to be as tiny and timid as the Wizard of Oz.

There he was, the President of India, behind serried ranks of security, behind facades inspired by the forts of the Maharajahs. Of all the people I met in India, he was the most Gandhian. And, dare I say, the most lovable. And he was also an Untouchable. From the hovels of the outcasts he's become the first citizen, the man who lives on Delhi's Raisina Hill.

Fifty years after nationhood around 15 per cent of the Indian population — 150 million people — are still cast, or perhaps caste, into the outer darkness of untouchability. The term 'Untouchable' is, these days, politically incorrect, like calling an African-American a black, a Negro or, worse still, a nigger. Even 'Harijan', the name promoted by Gandhi, has been abandoned. To be characterised as 'children of God' is now seen as patronising, implying that people are passive objects of pity. So the preferred term is found in the bureaucratic classification of 'scheduled castes', referring to the schedule which after Independence, gave Untouchables special consideration for parliamentary seats and public employment. But the more aggressive, separatist and politicised Untouchables refer to themselves as Dalit as, increasingly, does the media.

Despite the schedule, and despite Gandhi's campaign to improve their lot, Dalits are overwhelmingly poor and still endure systematic oppression in the cities and villages where, frequently, they're not permitted to share water or other communal facilities. The majority are landless agricultural workers, while others slave in the quarries, pull the rickshaws or work in the stench of the tanneries. Or they burn the bodies on the *ghats*. There is nothing 'under' about Indian undertaking — bodies are given to the sky and to the water. But it remains a Dalit profession.

There seems to be increasing violence against the Dalits. To some extent the rising figures are a consequence of Dalits having the courage to report incidents, but there are also attacks from workers and landowners in response to the Dalits' demands for equal pay and land distribution.

The radicalised Dalits are increasing their political influence through the Bahujana Samaj Party (which translates as 'the party of the common people'). And with the provisions for scheduled castes guaranteeing 4 per cent of representation in Parliament, they're becoming a force to be reckoned with. The BSP is now in an unholy alliance with the BJP, and the Dalits' insistence that they have the same civil rights as, for example, the Brahmins, has led to fierce and retributive attacks by higher caste Indians.

The first political stirrings of the Untouchables came in the early 1930s when B. R. Ambedkar harnessed their power while, at the same time, suggesting they convert to Buddhism in an attempt to escape from the tyranny of the caste system. (Ambedkar was one of the principal people involved in drafting the constitution in 1930–1931. He insisted on 'reservations' for oppressed castes.) These days such conversions are rare — the Dalits' social progress being propelled by improvements in education. Where 6 per cent of Dalit women were literate 1971, and 9 per cent of men, around 40 per cent are literate today. Increasing numbers of Dalits have found their way to the cities where they mingle and merge with the other castes. As Oliver Mendelssohn, co-author of *The Untouchables: Subordination, Poverty and the State in Modern India* told me, 'You cannot choose whom you wish to sit next to on a Delhi bus.'

I arrive at the palace while India is at the height of its political crisis. Putative prime ministers queue for an audience. Everything else is off the President's agenda. No ribbons will be cut, no trees planted and no diplomats, not even from nations of the most awesome power, may present their credentials. Suddenly the President is truly powerful, not simply a ceremonial figure but the architect of national destiny.

Yet, to the astonishment of our High Commissioner and the chagrin of a host of journalists, the President agrees to see me. True, it requires some delicate negotiations, the provision of a carefully modulated CV and a proposed line of questioning. Nonetheless the official invitation comes as a surprise, and is closely examined for fear of it being a forgery.

But I'm not surprised. I know that the President is fond of Australia, he was acting High Commissioner in his youth and returned, years later, as a Minister for Science on an official visit. We have a mutual friend in Barry Jones, who was his opposite number in the Hawke government.

The newspapers are full of the President's problems and dilemmas. 'He must deal with a fractured mandate and a shattered polity. He consults with the law ministry, the Attorney-General, the Solicitor-General, editors, intellectuals, retired judges, and has, finally, made his decision.'

'Never in the history of the republic has the head of state agonised for so long to put in place "a government that commands". Back in 1979, 1990, 1991, 1996 the situations were different as smaller parties, with the support of larger parties, were able to muster the simple or absolute majority.'

'This time a large party has had to try desperately to lasso others, and even as the new Prime Minister basks in the fusillade of camera flashes, there are many who believe that he'll lose the first confidence motion.'

It was only a moment ago that the Untouchables — whatever you call them, and they've been called lots of names before Dalit, including paravans and pariahs — were expected to crawl backwards with a broom sweeping their footprints so that Brahmins would not defile themselves by accidentally stepping where they had stepped. As Arundhati Roy writes: 'Paravans were not allowed to walk on public roads, not allowed to cover their upper bodies, not allowed to carry umbrellas. They had to put their hands over their mouths when they spoke, to divert their polluted breath away from those whom they addressed.'

It wasn't only the Buddhist faith that accepted Dalit converts. Arundhati Roy describes Dalits being Christianised in Kerala and, therefore, officially made casteless. 'It was like having to sweep away your footprints without a broom. Or worse, not being *allowed* to leave footprints at all.'

But even when Paravans, Pelayas and Pulayas joined the Anglican Church they could not escape the scourge of untouchability. 'As added incentive they were given a little food and money,' writes Roy in *The God of Small Things*.

> They were known as the rice-Christians. It didn't take them long to realise that they'd jumped from the frying pan into the fire. They were made to have separate churches with separate services and separate priests. As a special favour they were even given their own separate Pariah bishop. But after Independence they found they were not entitled to any government benefits like job reservations or bank loans at low interest rates.

Despite the attempts of Gandhi, and others, to wipe out the caste system, it endures. The fact that a Dalit lives where the viceroys lived may smack of the miraculous, but it does not mean the caste system has been cast aside. The First Citizen is, first and foremost, the rule-proving exception.

And isn't that the great thing about a republican system? It's not so much the reserve powers of the President, his constitutional ability to sack a recalcitrant prime minister, as his reserve imagery. Thus a Mary Robinson can give the politics of the Irish Republic a glow, an international cachet, that the system doesn't deserve. The President can be a paradox, a contradiction, camouflage. In some ways this has been the case with Australia's incumbent Governor-General whose decency, compassion and detestation of bigotry has set him apart, almost dangerously so, from the Howard government.

We are here to meet the paradox. We flash our invitation at the guards at the perimeter, by the vast wrought-iron gates that mark the first line of power and defence. We are led through gateway after gateway, through gates of the magnitude seen guarded by St Peter in cartoons about Heaven, and are rushed towards the second line of security where, quite understandably in this land of assassinations, we're asked to pass through an airport-style metal detector. But it's a model of such electronic decrepitude that it wouldn't have beeped had I had the Welcome Stranger stuffed up my skivvy. I walk through it twice in the hope of rekindling its interest but it gives the electronic counterpart to a shrug. However my camera excites some attention and is all but dismantled. Now the security guy insists on doing the same thing with the video camera. But we don't have a video camera, I explain. This is a tape recorder. Then where is your video camera? We don't have a video camera. I'm here to interview the President for the wireless.

Everything grinds to a halt. There are some muttered conversations among the officials. Then it becomes quite clear that we're not going to get in unless we have a video camera which can be closely examined. So I admit to error, confessing that the tape recorder is, in fact, a video camera. With smiles of relief the device is prodded and poked at. And, with good grace, we are passed on to a bloke from protocol.

The President, like the Pope, has the most marvellous private gardens to wander through and to think in, while he cogitates on his constitutional crisis. There's a round garden and a rectangular garden, each of excruciating formality, and a garden where, thanks to pruning of military precision, there are topiary elephants. And you realise that the presidential palace, every bit as much as the little garden where the Mahatma was murdered, is another Gandhian theme park.

It's clear that we're now close to the private quarters and one wonders whether we're within cooee of the bedrooms where Lady Mountbatten enjoyed hanky-panky with Nehru, in a tryst that, history suggests, had at least a diagonal nod from her husband, the last Viceroy, who was as attracted to the Indian leader as his missus. If these walls could only speak.

And they do, loud and clear, but the subject is not that *ménage à trois* but the singular figure of Gandhi. For he is here at every step of the way. Oh, there's a simply enormous white marble statue of a dancing, multi-armed *Shiva*, vast and octopoidal. Nonetheless, like Christ in the Vatican, like Walt at Disneyland, it is the bent figure of Gandhi that dominates. We pass statue after statue, painting after painting. Gandhi sits, Gandhi prays, Gandhi strides, Gandhi gazes. In stone, in bronze, in oils.

But Gandhi's red, concrete footsteps have long since disappeared and the yellow brick road is now a red carpet. The flunkies, the aides-de-camp in their summer uniforms with gold braid epaulets, lead me into the presidential presence — a gracious room dominated by books, leather-bound editions of Dickens, Robert Louis Stevenson, Joseph Conrad. But there is no Naipaul, neither Shiva nor V.S., no books written by anyone called Vithran and most emphatically no Salman Rushdie. As in all libraries of this type, the bookcases soar and the shelves buckle beneath the weight of tonnes of tomes in leather bindings. The spines are as neatly aligned as the presidential guards parading in their uniforms. And just as the guards are rarely called upon to shoot anyone, the books have rarely been opened. Though the current President, the tenth, was educated in British literature, I doubt that he's touched them. But perhaps the Mountbattens browsed through them.

I note the names of other British authors, obscure and forgotten, and that the fine leather bindings have been besmirched by catalogue numbers, little Dewey decimal registrations vandalising the pristine spines.

While waiting for the President to materialise I begin to count the images of Gandhi in this most innermost of sanctums. One, two, three, four ... plus the gold record on the wall. A gold record? I examine the little plaque — it's a recording of Gandhi's speeches.

Poor Gandhi. Loved by the people, killed by the fanatics, appropriated by the powerful. And about as relevant to what's going on in India today as Joan of Arc to Chirac or Boadicea to Blair.

The British may have left India but British forms still apply in this place, this palace, with aides-de-camp in British-style uniforms and the strict observation of British-style protocols. But the Britishness of it all evaporates when the aides open the door and the President appears. In fact, he almost disappears as he enters. He is that small, that self-effacing, that quiet. Yet, like so many of the elderly leaders of his country, the President glows with health, managing to look at least a decade younger than his seventy-seven years.

There is a familiar idealism in the way he talks of his country and its polity that seems remote from the reality, for the politics outside this building (and in recent hours within it) are as ruthless as any on Earth. Tammany Hall is alive and well and living in Delhi. The right-wing faction of the NSW Labor Party would feel at home. And beyond the endless argy-bargy lies the powder keg of communal tensions, just waiting for a casual or calculated match. The serenity in this room, and in this man, cannot be found in India's democracy, which was born in ethnic cleansing, with the death of a million or more, and continues to be threatened by communal violence — at least 20,000 significant upheavals since Independence.

A small, exquisite man with an uncertain smile, at once wary and warm, the President takes my hands in his — and I am shocked by his touch because his skin is soft and silken. It's a long time since he held a broom to sweep away his footsteps.

We sit in deep chairs and sip tea from bone china from a silver tray. The talk begins. I remind him that Australia is considering employing a local as head of state. Is being president of a modern nation a job he'd recommend?

He makes the appropriate response. 'Somebody should be head of state, there are advantages to having a head of state, for the sense of unity of the country, for someone objective and not directly involved in all the divisions and controversies of politics.'

I ask about the protocols of appointment. India uses an electoral college rather than a popular vote. 'Yes, I was elected by members of Parliament of both houses and by the legislators of the states. And yes, like me, the other nine presidents came from the world of politics. Almost all of them were important leaders, though the second president was not an active participant in the national movement but a distinguished academic, writer, philosopher. And we had another who was also a great educationalist.

'No, we did not consider direct election. Views were expressed in a constitutional assembly, but there was no majority support. During the last ten years political scientists and politicians have expressed the view that a popular election of the president might be suitable for India. But it has not gathered momentum.'

I talk of the red footsteps marking Gandhi's last walk. 'Are you still walking in them?'

'Not exactly. But we're certainly remembering him, particularly in critical times. Then Gandhi becomes very relevant to India and people recall him. It is difficult to walk in the footsteps of a man like that. He was a great man, extraordinary man, and his influence is pervasive in the Indian mind. Even those who do not agree with him have been affected by his example.'

I gesture around the room — Gandhi's face is everywhere, on the currency, on the walls. But the President denies that he's been deified. 'Oh, some of his followers have tried, but people follow him, follow his ideas, after rational thinking.'

Now he talks of his own life. His father was a physician, working in traditional medicine. 'A stream of education ran through my family. And in spite of all the social divisions and discriminations of society at that time, there was one government primary school which enabled me to have an education ... and there was an English middle school in the village, about two kilometres from my own house, run by the Catholic Church. So after primary school, I could go to the English school.

'No, there were absolutely no concessions. But primary education was free, except for books and incidental expenses. But middle school was a private school, and the Church provided half of the costs. Then I went to high school, what they called higher secondary, and that was further away from my village, nearly 5 kilometres from my home. I did well in high school, and that made all the difference in my career because I got a scholarship and therefore could think of going to college. That was 20 kilometres from my home. But very soon, after a month, I found that I could not afford to pay for meals, so I was really thinking of returning home, when someone introduced me to a gentleman who was a government leader in the city. And each day he gave me lunch and dinner in his home which enabled me to survive.'

Why had he chosen to study British literature?

'I was interested in literature as such, in the literature of my own language. But English literature was more systematically taught, so I elected to study it. I then became a newspaper cadet with a Hindu newspaper and then managed to get to London and the London School of Economics.

'Yes, it was extraordinary. The war was still going on. So scholarships were not being given at that time. But I got one because I had a good degree. The war was still on when I left Bombay, and Germany's surrender took place when our boat was at Port Said.'

'And you returned from London with a letter from Professor Lasky to Nehru ... a letter that gave you the opportunity to be a diplomat?'

'Yes. That is true. I had no ambition or desire to be a diplomat, or even a government servant. I would have been happy to be a teacher at the university, or a journalist. Those were my ambitions. But the professor's letter to Nehru changed everything. And I had a very enjoyable posting in Australia as First Secretary in our High Commission, and was acting High Commissioner most of the time. The High Commissioner was heavily involved in Indochina, so I held the fort. So I have very pleasant memories of Australia. And many friends in Australia.

'I remember my daughter being interviewed by the ABC. "How do you like Canberra?" she was asked. She said, "I like it very much, it is full of gumtrees".'

We talked of the parallels between Canberra and Delhi. The official cities date from the same time, and both were works of single expatriate architects. The most significant difference is that Delhi has more gumtrees.

'You married a Burmese woman. I understand that you needed permission from Nehru for this marriage.'

'In those days, soon after independence, we were intensely nationalistic, so our foreign service was also nationalistic. Naturally we wanted to show Indian womanhood abroad, and therefore there was a rule that nobody should marry foreigners, and if they did, they should send in their resignation. But Nehru was kind and understand in our case.'

He talked of difficult jobs, difficult situations, difficult times, the tasks of repairing relationships with China after years of friction, of attempting to fix the relationship with the US after a period when India's role leading the non-aligned nations had made Washington very angry. 'In both countries relations did normalise themselves and improve. And it gave me preparation and an education for this job.'

How had he made the move from diplomacy to politics?

'It was a conscious decision. When I returned from the United States I retired. I found myself doing nothing except writing to newspapers. I needed a job, something to do. Perhaps this is a normal thing for people who are unemployed — they get involved in politics. And at that time Mrs Gandhi declared elections and I went to her and asked if I could get a ticket, and she was good enough to find a ticket for me in my home state. I became Vice President of India from 1992 to 1997 which also meant that I was Speaker of the Upper House.'

'And because you were respected by all sides, you were anointed President. What was the reaction of people across India to the knowledge that you'd risen from the lowest of the castes?'

'Oh, there was some displeasure. But by and large I was amazed by the reaction. Particularly the reaction of the ordinary man, some of whom were excited by the possibility that an ordinary fellow could become head of state. It was something to give them hope.'

'Are they still entitled to have that hope?'

'Oh yes. Certainly. The caste system has been battered really heavily during these last fifty years. Though politics, political parties and politicians, have found a weapon in the caste system and therefore appealed to caste emotions for getting votes. So this has given a new lease of life in the political periphery. It may look as if caste has become strengthened. But it is not so. Its social basis, its economic basis, has been undermined considerably by developments after independence. Caste is much weaker in a fundamental sense today, though it is displayed very conspicuously at the political level.'

I pointed to one of the statues of Gandhi. 'I understand that you met Gandhi, but it was on one of his silent days?'

'I didn't know what to do. Then they said, "You can still ask questions, Gandhi will answer your questions." To make my situation more difficult, he was eating his lunch, with all the leaders of India around him. It was a formidable experience. There he was, with the great leaders, eating chapatti and vegetables, but I still asked my questions. And he put his plate of chapattis aside, took a pencil, and scribbled the answers.'

'Do you still have those scribbled answers?'

'I have got them. I've got them. Though it is fading. When I was in Australia I had them photostatted and they also did something, put powder on them, to keep it clear. It is still readable.'

Again he takes my hand in his. Again I am touched by the Untouchable and the touch is soft, gentle and tender. He holds my hands for a long time and now his smile is unequivocally warm. We pose for the obligatory photographs, standing beneath yet another portrait of Gandhi who gazes down on us through his rimless spectacles. His eyes on the man in the eye of the storm.

The President looks into my eyes as if I were his oldest friend or the returning prodigal. No wonder he was so successful as a diplomat, so loved as a politician. And now, so revered as First Citizen.

A little later we watch him swearing in the new Cabinet. One of the most memorable appointments is that of Jayaram Jayalalitha, a former Chief Minister of the Southern Tamil Nadu state who likes to be known as a 'walking goddess'.

Walking goddess is just one of the many titles she's adopted. She's likes to be known, as well, as a revolutionary leader, a female deity and a guardian angel. I'm looking forward to meeting her, to suggest yet another title: the dominatrix of New Delhi.

After completing her first year in office she sat on a silver throne wearing a jewel-studded gold crown while millions, yes *millions*, of party workers filed past her in the temple town of Madurai.

The men in her party are expected to prostrate themselves before her when admitted to her presence. Scores of supporters have her name tattooed on their arms or on the back of their hands as a mark of loyalty.

Jayaram Jayalalitha once hosted a wedding lunch for around 150,000 of her most intimate friends, the spread spread over 12 hectares. Her birthdays are invariably elaborate affairs. Now fifty, she celebrated her forty-seventh birthday by encouraging hundreds of her devotees to walk on fire, in a deep trench outside a temple in Madras that had been filled with two tonnes of coal and firewood.

Her senior party members compete with one another to devise ecstatic celebrations for her. One became a contest to indulge her belief in the magical powers of number nine.

According to press reports it took place on 27 January (2 + 7 = 9) in three separate marriage halls in Madras numbered, 27, 36 and 126, each of which adds up, yes, to nine. It had taken nine party members nine days to find the three halls. Nine state ministers attended the event to which nine colleagues from nine districts were invited. Her preference for the number led her to have a 27-member Cabinet. All meetings were held on the ninth or a date divisible by nine.

Given her passion for numerology it is not surprising that Prime Minister Vajpayee has not awarded her a financial ministry.

5

Poverty

I walk the streets of Mumbai with P. Sainath, the strikingly handsome and passionately idealistic young journalist who I've come to know from his contributions to 'Late Night Live'. The words come pouring out.

PA: Tell me about the BJP victory.

PS: Nothing very much has happened. A party that had 161 seats now has 176 seats. The supposed victory is mainly achieved by alliances. The BJP was anti-federal. By accepting the kinds of allies it has it's been forced to acknowledge that this country is getting to be more and more federal. That is perhaps the most significant development. But we see one of the most fragile coalitions of all time.

PA: Will it last longer than thirteen days?

PS: Yes, the Prime Minister would be hard put to break his own record. But it's not even a coalition. It's a coalition of coalitions. In many states, they've gone into alliance with a group of parties. The negotiations were preposterously complex, their letter to the President of India delayed because everyone was demanding their price. 'We want this portfolio. We want the Finance portfolio. We want the Housing portfolio.' So a party that has criticised coalition politics consistently has now been forced to accept their reality.

POVERTY 63

PA: The Congress Party couldn't have pulled a coalition together?

PS: The Congress Party grew too accustomed to being the party of governors. They couldn't think of alliance politics. The one place where they acquiesced was in this state, Maharashtra, of which Mumbai is the capital. For once they accepted that they were not the all-dominant, all-powerful party they once were. They went in for alliance politics here and swept the state.

PA: Why didn't they extrapolate from that success?

PS: Ah, the Congress culture! They're very greedy. They're extremely greedy. It's deeply rooted in their nature. When a party's been in power for forty years they're not willing to share. They must be top banana.

PA: Yet the party's been declining since 1977.

PS: Yes. But it made a huge comeback in 1984, after the assassination of Mrs Gandhi. And in 1991 the assassination of Rajiv Gandhi saved it from complete obliteration.

PA: Has it been enfeebled by its dynastic connections?

PS: Dynastic politics gave Congress its momentum for many, many years. But lately they've been adopting policies that have driven away their natural constituency. The Congress was a huge coalition of various class forces. It had the tribal and indigenous people. It had the minorities, particularly the Muslims, who trusted the Congress as a secular party. And it had the Untouchables, the scheduled castes.

PA: A broad church, as we say in the West.

PS: A very broad church. And in the freedom struggle, it was the broadest of churches. But now many of its traditional supporters, particularly the poor, have been alienated by Congress.

PA: The new Prime Minister represents himself as a great warrior in the war of independence against the Brits. But it seems that it ain't necessarily so. There are accusations that he was, in effect, a collaborator with the British and named names. One could draw parallels with the Vichy French.

PS: What he did was falsify his role in the freedom struggle. And he's forced to confess his affiliations. But at the same time he's denied any wrongdoing.

PA: A bit like Bill Clinton saying 'I didn't inhale'.

PS: Exactly. A lot of people have run away from a lot of battles and lots of people have lots to hide. But in the 1980s our new Prime Minister wrote articles about his role in the Quit India Movement that are simply nonsensical.

PA: Yet the Indian newspapers are full of lickspittle editorials in which he's characterised as some sort of saint. A mixture of Mahatma Gandhi and Mother Teresa.

PS: The upper middle classes just love him, and the press dotes on him, despite the revelations about his past.

We tread warily around a family lying unconscious on the footpath, a woman with a couple of young children.

PA: Let's talk about poverty in India. What are the statistics?

PS: The government has abandoned the 19 per cent estimate. 'Let's get rid of that rubbish,' said a former Finance Minister, 'it's making a laughing stock of us.' So we've thrown out that 19 per cent estimate and acknowledge that, by government parameters, about 40 per cent of the Indian people live below the official poverty line.

PA: That's a bold step for a government. In our country, for example, officials keep doctoring the figures to minimise the unemployment statistics.

PS: We still doctor the figures. We have studies that come out which are ludicrous. I've been looking at one which claimed to have over 300 parameters in surveying respondents below the poverty line. I met the guy who did the study, for a big multinational and said, 'I'm a professional journalist and I do interviews for a living.

I'd like to know how you ever asked anyone 300 questions. Because if you did, your respondents would die of fatigue, not of hunger.' Let's be very clear. In India, the official standard of poverty does not take into account factors like health, education, sanitation, ownership of assets. None of this. None! Nor is literacy calculated in the poverty statistics. It is not taken as an official indicator.

PA: But it should be part of a multifactorial equation, surely?

PS: Absolutely. If you look at the United Nations' Human Development Report you'll find a very different picture of India than the one that the leadership of this country projects. You'll see that in quality of life, India is below El Salvador, a country that's been at civil war forever.

PA: You write scathingly honest accounts of Indian politics. You are also reckless in your analysis of the ultra-right.

PS: Yes, the likes of Mr Baltakri who makes the BJP seem moderate. He would make Pauline Hanson sound like a left-wing liberal. You'd be frightened to hear him speak.

PA: I'm frightened already.

PS: I've good reason to be afraid. My office has been smashed three times by his goon over the past few years. Any journalist has good reason to be frightened. In this state physical attacks on journalists and newspaper offices occur constantly. Baltakri's mob consists of a large number of unemployed youths whose despair, whose absolute despair about the future, leads them to thuggery. The city saw the closure of mills, textile mills, in the 1980s, throwing hundreds of thousands of workers out of jobs. The pressures have been building ever since. Throughout Mumbai you see the emergence of gated communities, the sorts of things you find in the Philippines and California. If you go to Delhi you're going to see a lot of residential colonies protected by steel gates. You're seeing the sneaking privatisation of public property.

PA: But they open the gates to let the domestics in. And middle-class life is made tolerable, pleasurable, luxurious because of the remarkably low cost of labour.

PS: Yes, a situation made worse by the gigantic subsidies that the wealthy get in this country. We run the biggest welfare state for the wealthy in the world.

PA: And for the wealthy it's imperative to have slums, to house their servants.

PS: Absolutely. You have a state whose activity, whose policies, are geared towards enriching and enhancing the lives of the top 10 per cent. Let me give you two quick snapshots which will tell you what's happened in the last five or six years. At the end of 1997 three television channels had reports on fraud in India's health clinics. Between 1991 and 1996 we've had hundreds of clinics opening up to fight obesity. Now, they were very well investigated reports. They showed people being given pills for a few thousand *rupees* that made you lose weight temporarily — but you soon doubled your weight and there were serious side effects and problems. Now, I must admit to being rather entertained by this; the thought of thousands of Indians battling to lose weight. During the same periods hundreds of millions of Indians had less food to eat. The press was talking about the problems of Indians fighting obesity when the amount of food available per Indian had declined sharply. In 1991 the average Indian was having access to 510 grams of food grain. By 1995 that was down to 461. That's one snapshot.

PA: Apart from the poor themselves, is anyone really interested in destroying poverty in this country?

PS: Yes. A motley group of political forces is interested. But I don't think they've been able to get their act together. Nonetheless there are parts of India which have done some of the basics required to break poverty. I do not believe it would cost a lot of money to end poverty in India. Let us look at a couple of processes that are under way. You know, fundamentalist forces like the Muslim League and the BJP are nothing to the number one fundamentalism in the world today — market fundamentalism. What you're seeing in our cities is the result of policies that are leading to casualisation of labour, to tremendous insecurity at the lower levels of society. And here is the second snapshot for you. Look at the cover stories of magazines over the past five years and there are the CEOs of India, being paid record salaries while the wages of labourers and agricultural workers, urban and rural, have been falling. So at one end of the spectrum there are people getting salaries that have never been heard of in this country. And at the other? People who are suffering a real erosion of living standards. It's a recipe for disaster.

PA: Let's measure poverty in another way. Let's factor in land ownership.

PS: Let's put this question: in India, who are the poor? Forty per cent of the poor are landless agricultural labourers. Forty-five per cent of them are small marginal farmers. Over 60 per cent of Indian farmers own less than one acre of land. So that's 85 per cent of your people. 7.5 per cent are rural artisans, in the non-farm sector. And all the others form the remaining 7.5 per cent. As a matter of fact, the rate of growth of urban poverty has been faster than the rate of growth of rural poverty.

PA: And what about health?

PS: The social sector investments in this country are declining as the size of the problem has been expanding. Excepting in the communist states, 85 per cent of health expenses in this country are privately borne by the citizens themselves. Our health expenditure as a share of gross domestic product is one of the lowest in the world.

PA: What of education?

PS: In this country you're talking about 70 to 100 million children who do not go to school.

At this point a group of beggar children surrounded us, with upturned palms and requests for money.

PS: Yes, Mumbai has very many of them, despite its boasts of being such a rich city. Let me give you a picture of how this happens. Out of every 100 children of school age, 70 are actually enrolled. So 30 are eliminated immediately. Out of those 70 who enter class one, 35 drop out by class five. So you're left with 35. Of the remaining 35, all but ten drop out by class eight. So by the time you complete high school you're left with just five of the original 100.

PA: That's a terrible waste. I was talking this morning to some of the kids hustling on the esplanade. I befriended a little bloke who called himself Bob. He was nine-years-old, energetic, street-smart, a delightful little kid. He told me he'd been out of school now for eighteen months. It's a waste.

PS: Absolutely. But you can look at it two ways. As I said, you're left with just five kids at the high school level out of the original 100. You can look at the system as being 95 per cent inefficient. Or you can look at it as a system that is 95 per cent efficient, in that it weeded out the undesirable. That's the view that many choose to take.

PA: One of the things you inherited from the British was bureaucracy. And Indians seem to have a natural aptitude for it. You would have thought that with all your bureaucrats things would be more efficient.

PS: Indian society is incredibly over-bureaucratised. I've been staying at a hotel where they've organised the satellite dish so that when you turn on your 40-channel TV you can see only one channel. Why? Because some bureaucrat said, 'Nobody watches more than one channel at a time. So why spoil the TV by letting people flick the channels. It will wear out the buttons.'

PA: My experience at Mumbai airport was typical. To simply catch a taxi into town required me dealing with no less than seven bureaucrats. They passed me from person to person with much filling out of forms to catch a taxi! Well, I suppose it helps tackle poverty.

PS: There are many people with no work to do. None. They become the fringe elements. So they want to pick up your bags and move them a couple of feet. These are able-bodied people who would far prefer to have real jobs.

PA: What about infant mortality rates?

PS: They vary dramatically. In Uttar Pradesh there's an infant mortality rate of over 100 per 1000. But in Kerala infant mortality is about the same as the United States. But the more babies that die, the more babies will be born. Because an average Indian peasant couple in the north of India, in the Hindi heartland, want to have two children alive. To look after them in their old age. So they need to have six children in the first place.

PA: What is it in the Indian psyche, in the social structure, that prevents revolutionary outrage?

PS: People are dislocated, not united. They're in different regions which are so far apart. Oh, there are frequent outbursts of rage. I believe that a third of this country is on the verge of serious conflict. Or what a senior bureaucrat has actually called 'conditions of low intensity civil war'. I believe that's true.

PA: But isn't a lot of this religious conflict?

PS: No. In Bihar or Uttar Pradesh it has to do with people fighting for land.

PA: Is caste still a determining factor in poverty?

PS: In poverty, no. Nonetheless there is a great correspondence in the countryside between caste and class. But it's not a one-to-one correspondence. You do find certain castes at the bottom of the heap, but you also find an aristocracy within those castes.

PA: And genteel poverty emerging in the middle class?

PS: Some sections have never had it so good. But those on fixed incomes are losing out.

PA: Could the euphoric editorials be right? Could the BJP government tackle India's problems, particularly the problem of poverty, more effectively that the corrupt, exhausted Congress?

PS: Out of the question. The evidence stares you in the face. Firstly, in the history of India, no BJP government has ever completed a five-year term. They are the most unstable people in the history of governance. Secondly, whenever they have ruled, wherever they've been in government, they've been massively rejected at a subsequent election. There's invariably a backlash within three years. That happened in Maharashtra and in Rajistan.

PA: If caste isn't the determinant of poverty, what about religion? Is there a fundamental difference between the poverty level of Muslim and Hindu?

PS: The Muslims, the minorities as a whole, are poor. There's no question about that. Nonetheless you have fabulously rich sections within the Muslim community.

PA: What about the Dalits?

PS: The word literally means 'oppressed'. When you say 'I'm Dalit, I'm an oppressed person', you're also marking out the existence of an oppressor.

PA: It sounds a bit fashionable, doesn't it? The claim of victimhood.

PS: The Dalit stream represents the most militant of tendencies within these communities. Those who are lashing out at oppression. The ones who are fighting it. It's a very divided, very fractured stream.

PA: The President was born into an Untouchable family.

PS: He's very exceptional. There are over 450 such groups in this country. They're often severely divided internally, in bitter conflict with each other. So you do still have people calling themselves Harijans. And in the deep south, some describe themselves as 'SC'. But in the west of India and North India increasingly people are calling themselves Dalit.

PA: A rose is a rose is a rose. Are they overcoming the problems inherited at the time of Partition?

PS: They're very far from overcoming them.

PA: How many Indians would be members of the scheduled castes?

PS: There are more Dalits in India than there are people in Pakistan; 160 million of them. 16.48 per cent of our population if you want to be precise.

PA: And where do they fit into the Hindu cosmology?

PS: They were outside the caste system. They were literally outcasts. They were subjected to enormous barbarities. Their lands were seized. They formed the largest number of the army of landless, India's poorest people.

PA: And they were allowed to operate in professions deemed unclean.

PS: Allowed is a terrible word. They were compelled. They might be compelled to look after the sanitation of a village. And they were not allowed to touch anything else.

PA: They were the shit-kickers.

PS: Exactly.

PA: They worked in tanneries. What else?

PS: They looked after the burning *ghats*. The washing, the laundry. They performed every kind of menial task for the landlords, for the upper castes. And they had to observe rules. Suppose a Brahmin was walking. A person below the Brahmin caste had to walk a fixed distance from him. A person below the second caste had to walk at a fixed distance from that person. And the Dalit, if he saw these people coming, had to hide at the side of the street so that he did not pollute their fair shadow.

PA: I recognise that there are many dialects in India, many immensely powerful languages. You find Hindi in New Delhi, for example, Bengali in Bengal. Sainath, is there any way that a member of a scheduled caste can be identified by the way they speak? Irrespective of language? I'm thinking of Britain, of course, where class is clearly defined by the use of English — as Shaw's Professor Higgins reminds us.

PS: People from the upper caste in Uttar Pradesh, for example, can spot such a person at a glance. And the guy who sells food outside my office spotted me as a Brahmin straightaway. And after that I used to try and challenge him. I'd bring friends along and say, 'What is this guy?' It used to infuriate me that he always got it right.

PA: How did he do it?

PS: I don't know how.

PA: So people in India can tell.

PS: Those who invented the system, they seem to be able to tell. I don't think an urban Indian can really tell. But in rural India you can tell almost by the posture, by the attitudes, the behaviour.

PA: So it's not so much in the voice. It's in the body language after a few thousand years.

PS: Yes, but it's breaking down. Particularly in the north given the movement towards self-respect. I'd been living for several weeks in Dalit communities and that reinforced my faith in electoral democracy. The authorities were so anti-Dalit that they organised the voting booths in a special way. In the Dalit ghetto there were 219 voters. Next to us were 350 upper-caste voters. The polling booth for the upper-caste voters was placed among them, for their convenience. The polling booth for Dalits? Four kilometres away across a dirt track. So anyone who wanted to vote had to walk eight kilometres! But, Phillip, every one of them did. Including a seventy-six-year-old woman. She walked that four kilometres and voted and walked four kilometres back. Because she saw it as a chance of calling the powerful to account.

PA: Let's go back to the notion of scheduling. The scheduled castes are given special consideration in government and in jobs, are they not?

PS: Yes, what the West calls affirmative action. There are government jobs for the scheduled classes and the scheduled tribes. It's a fine thing. I'm supportive of it. Nonetheless it's a bandaid. And there's a huge problem, given that most of the scheduled castes don't complete school or college.

PA: The idea of affirmation action is suffering a backlash in the West.

PS: And here, too. In the most unjustifiable manner. No, affirmative action doesn't solve everything. But it's a psychological help.

PA: One of the things that surprises, even shocks upper-class people around the world is the vibrancy found in the working class. Again and again we see the working class energising a culture in a way that the affluent cannot. Look at the cultural contribution that flows from the American ghettos. That came, for example, from the Beatles in Liverpool. Is there a cultural energy, an intellectual energy, coming from the Dalits?

PS: The cultural energy from the tribals and the Dalits has always been phenomenal. They form a quarter of the country's population and do a great deal of its work. At the same time, many of the most wonderful things you will see in Indian culture derived from the Dalits and the tribes. But their share of education … disastrously low.

PA: Isn't that where you really need scheduling? At the educational level?

PS: Absolutely. Education should be universal. But the Indian elite are very happy and comfortable with child labour, Phillip. It's a form of contemporary slavery. There's no other word for it.

PA: When I was growing up Australians thought of India with fascinated horror. It was the country where you could step over the bodies of the dying or the dead on the streets. And we were so proud of our own culture, our economic triumphs. These days, of course, people live in cardboard boxes in post-Thatcherite London, and Melbourne and Sydney have a great many street kids. Behold the operation of free market forces. So we all share these problems.

PS: India is a very peculiar package. It's not a sub-Saharan African state. You no longer find people dying in the streets. What you do have is a more difficult kind of poverty and a more difficult kind of hunger. In the countryside, for example, what you're going to see is not the squalor of the city but something almost invisible. An invisible hunger. Five hundred calories less than you need.

PA: On previous trips to India I've observed a passivity in people, a stillness. As I've wandered around the country I've noticed people staring without rancour or curiosity. And it occurred to me that it was a symptom of being undernourished.

PS: That's exactly what I'm talking about. For instance, a child who's getting, say, a third less than he or she needs might look normal. But there is serious physiological and perhaps psychological damage.

POVERTY 75

PA: There's been a belated acknowledgment by many of the Christian churches that they were guilty of everything from cultural imperialism to economic colonialism. That the cross was as much a weapon as the sword. Now they're rethinking their theologies and trying to redeem themselves through social activism. I'm thinking of everything from the worker priests in Central America to the deep regrets expressed by Australian churches for their role, for example, in the 'stolen children' — the scandal of kidnapping kids from indigenous families. Leaving aside the zealotry of Hindu fundamentalists, has there been any movement within the Hindu faith to reconsider, to recast the whole notion of caste?

PS: There have been a large number of anti-class movements, some of them reformist in nature, some of them very militant in nature, for a very long time. Often they've been led by people from the upper classes. Hinduism is, of course, a very amorphous thing.

PA: Hinduism doesn't have a Vatican.

PS: No, although the BJP would like to create that kind of thing. And if you want to see where the BJP will take this country politically, if they can, which they can't, you have to cross the border into Pakistan. Oh, the tribal warfare! A non-tribal guy marries a tribal girl and you have 2000 people shooting it out. The BJP makes a demon out of Pakistan but it would like things to be pretty much like that.

PA: You are at once proud and despairing of your country.

PS: I'm not despairing. I'm angry.

PA: Whenever we speak on the wireless I hear, in your voice, a mixture of emotions: frustration, anger, righteous indignation. Yet you're finally optimistic that this extraordinary nation of a billion people, a billion anarchists, can hold itself together? Can make their democracy work?

PS: Absolutely. Everything these people have done in their history shows me that. These are the people who stopped the armies of Alexander. They turned them back. He couldn't go any further when he met the people in the north. That's where his career ended. You're right to speak about passivity. But the weak have their own weapons, their own ways of undermining you. You'll observe that at the traffic lights it's the bullock cart that gets its way. So I'm not despairing. I'm very proud to be an Indian and very proud to be an Indian journalist. You know, Phillip, the last time I was returning from Australia I was really homesick. And I'll tell you one of the things about Indian journalism that makes it remarkable, even at its worst. I boarded the plane at Singapore and, having read Australian papers for three months (forgive me, I won't say more than that), there was a *Times of India* headline about the beauty contests that were going on. And the headline read:

'PROTESTERS BITE POLICE IN BEAUTY CONTEST DRAW'.

I felt a rush of emotion! I felt I was going back to some real journalism!

PA: And to some real vitality.

PS: My neighbour was an Australian. He asked me, 'Would they really do that? Would they bite the police?' And I said, 'Don't you agree that we should have a law that allows citizens to bite police at frequent intervals? In that way we even things out.' He thought I was nuts. I could feel him physically withdrawing. But I thought it was a great headline.

PA: So even when you see Hindu fundamentalists on the march, even when you acknowledge the increase in communal rioting ...

PS: It frightens me. But I think it could be overcome. Remember that we had Partition rights in which one million people died. And a man called Gandhi gave his life — and that sacrifice kept this country free of communal rights for fourteen years. For fourteen years after the Mahatma gave his life!

PA: But Gandhis are thin on the ground.

PS: Yes, but there are many forces at the grassroots militating against fundamentalist tendencies. In fact, the BJP will confront forces it doesn't understand. Incidentally, look at this.

Sainath shows me photographs he's taken of temples completely painted over with Coca-Cola signs.

PA: So Coca-Cola are now into corporate sponsorship of shrines and temples? How marvellous.

PS: Isn't it just.

PA: Okay, here's a BJP policy that I approve of. Their determination to defend Indian culture from the predations of California.

PS: Fine. But what a pity the BJP has no understanding of the richness of Indian culture. Indian culture has survived for thousands of years before the BJP was around to damage it. Indian culture's done pretty well by itself, thank you very much. It's had an openness that's taken influences from all over the world. You have schools of art that are a mix of ancient Greek and Indian. You'll find Buddhism in Indian style.

PA: Yes, and the sari derives from the toga.

PS: Exactly. But if the BJP has its way, you'll have a dress code in this country. A country which has rich traditions in textiles and apparel. It is the diversity of this country's culture that makes the culture beautiful. But the BJP don't understand this.

PA: What draws the West to India is its polychromatic vitality. And you're suggesting the BJP are monochromatic, monocultural?

PS: Absolutely. They're very narrow in their outlook. I would be sympathetic to defending not just Indian culture but Australian culture — any culture — against Coca-Cola and the kind of values that go with it. But not the BJP way. If they succeed, they'll reduce the very great traditions to their meanest proportions. To the ideology of hatred.

PA: Let's circle back to poverty, because it boggles the mind. I have to say that everywhere in India I meet intelligent, educated, politically committed people who have been desensitised to it, who've become blind to it.

PS: The Indian elite and the Indian rich. I marvel at this. This is probably the only elite in the world that, on the one hand, makes money out of child labour, and then goes around to international forums collecting money to fight child labour. It goes to the United Nations to campaign for improved conditions of child labour. Yet, basically, they're happy with having the children of the poor work for them.

6

Mickey Spillane

I shuffle through the English language papers. Crime stories abound, reported in a style that seems heavily influenced by Mickey Spillane. People are 'bumped off', police are 'baffled'. And a typical story comes with a choice of headlines:

'TATTOO ON CORPSE MAKES COPS SCRATCH THEIR HEAD. COPS IN TIZZY OVER BODY.'

And here's another jewel.

A 30-year-old man was chased by some residents of Rajba colony in the wee hours, fell into a swamp and drowned. Thinking that he might be a thief, a resident of the area who was up and about had asked for his identity. The resident started chasing him and he called out to others. The fleeing man fell into a swamp. He struggled out but to no avail. In the morning fire brigade personnel pulled him out.

I'm puzzled about him struggling out 'to no avail'. Did they chase him back in again?

And I leaf through the classifieds — thousands upon thousands of people seeking brides or grooms. For example:

CONVENTED, Graduate, 3-year Course German, Pharmacist, Delhi Govt., own home, plot, unencumbered, non-smoker, teetotaller, gentle, handsome, Rajput, seeks well employed, qualified, blonde-n-beautiful woman of substance. Wanna love-n-spoil be loved-n-spoiled. Widow, divorcee welcome. Civil marriage acceptable. Box BT-6031-CA, *Hindustan Times*.

ALLIANCE invited from slim, smart, tall, fair, handsome, professional girl, preferably Medico for Punjabi Saraswat Brahmin, Public educated, fair, handsome, bachelor, 29/182/10,000, B.E. (Mech.), working Executive Engineer, Limited Company. Caste no bar for beautiful and meritorious girl. Apply full details through Box 37668-W, *Hindustan Times*.

SUITABLE match for beautiful, Punjabi girl, 25/152/ Graduate, with Hotel Management working abroad as manager in multinational company and living with family. Father Class One Offidcer, posted abroad on deputation. Person from status family preferably, educationist/ professionals/Defence need apply with full particulars. Early decent marriage. Box 37899-W, *Hindustan Times*.

ALLIANCE invited for Agarwal B.E. (Civil), MBA, 30/180/65, 39,000 p.m., own business from reputed Doc's family. Girl must be at least 160cm., slim with really attractive personality. Must be well educated, working/non-working from status family. Correspond A-37, Mount Kailash.

BEAUTIFUL, fair, slim caring, homely, without specs, height (152–157 cms) from status family for Punjabi Graduate boy, Public School background, 32/8500, Government employed. Girls want to settle out of Delhi only write. Preferably Central School Teachress/Bank employed. Box 37851-W, *Hindustan Times*.

ALLIANCE invited for pretty, brilliant, Punjabi, Arora girl, 23/157/21000 per month and accommodation, M.F.C., (equivalent MBA Finance), Delhi University, working on Software project with reputed American multinational at Mumbai. Box 108723-CA, *Hindustan Times*.

ALLIANCE invited from professionals/well settled businessmen for Punjabi Arora girl, Convent educated, B. Com., M.B.A., presently doing jewellery design/manufacturing course from reputed institution, beautiful, fair, sharp featured, 25/159. Father having well settled business in New Delhi. Box BA06976-CA, *Hindustan Times*.

The Indian Medici

A few weeks before leaving for India I received a phone call from Foreign Affairs in Canberra. Would I have time to meet a Mr O.P. Jain, a wealthy Indian visiting Australia to look at our cultural organisations? I remind the bureaucrat that I'm outside the loop these days, having resigned from all government postings, in the hope of protecting them from political vengeance. While it's understood that I'm not the most popular bloke with John Howard, the Department would, nonetheless, be grateful if I talked to Mr Jain about the history of the Australia Council, about the Victorian Council of the Arts, about the various film structures I've set up or chaired. So it's arranged he'll visit my home in Paddington.

O.P. Jain turns out to be one of the most elegant and patrician people I've ever met. He's poised, charming and exquisitely dressed, in classic Indian garb cut from khadi that seems to have been homespun from moonlight rather than silk. And his long, melancholy face and sweet-sad eyes recall Buster Keaton and Boris Pasternak. And he's accompanied by a sherpa from the Department who, to say the least, makes a dramatic contrast. His shirt is only half tucked into his trousers and a few popped buttons allow a vast belly to proclaim itself. Moreover, his zipper isn't entirely zipped.

The odd couple. And I get the feeling that O.P. Jain is more than a little embarrassed by his guide's appearance. But he is, of course, far too polite to complain.

I make a cuppa and pump him about his past. O.P. reveals that his family's fortune is based on the paper industry. For generations they made everything from bulk paper to the most exquisite handmade stationery. Now he wants to help his country by focusing on the arts. He shows me photographs of some beautiful building he's constructed over a large stretch of wasteland on the outskirts of Delhi, where artists can live in residence, painting their paintings, tossing their pots, writing their books. And he also wants to produce a new generation of arts administrators because most of India's artistic institutions — everything from theatrical companies to museums — are appallingly administered. He's determined to set up an overarching structure to save the plethora of India's cultural companies from themselves.

And here I am, a few weeks later, at the launch of O.P.'s Sanskriti Institute of Management for Cultural Organisations, an event attended by the *crème de la crème* of Delhi's political and diplomatic hierarchy. O.P. has managed to pull the American, the Austrian, the Japanese Ambassadors and the British and Australian High Commissioners. Senior ministers, high ranking bureaucrats and newspaper editors are also paying O.P. court. The evening begins with a succession of speeches from a distinguished panel. The first thing the Sanskriti Organisation will have to do is learn to control the people they put on their podia. While O.P.'s speech is modest, self-effacing and brief, his example is not followed by the others who, even without notes, waffle wonderfully, with the moral earnestness that characterises Indian public discourse.

(Indian society is full of people who dazzle with their intensity and eloquence. Yet their idealism doesn't seem to take effect. There's a lot of clutch-slipping in this society. The gears don't mesh. There's a cognitive dissidence between aspiration and achievement.)

But it's not only the length of the speeches that makes me fear for O.P.'s vision. It's the content. I'm recalling the lessons of thirty years spent in and around arts administration, dating back to the late 1960s when Nugget Coombs, Jean Battersby and Barry Jones were putting together the Australia Council, and of our teething troubles. I think of the history of a dozen newly established cultural bodies, recalling how we'd progressed by trial and error, mainly error. And the principal thing we'd learnt was that it was better to train artists to manage themselves than to bring managers in to manager artists. Look at the Literature Board, the least bureaucratised of any of the Oz Council's boards and, by any objective measure, the most successful.

When the speeches are over and everyone's having drinks I try to warn against a breeding program of arts managers, observing that they had a great ability to absorb dollops of money intended for artistic production. I spoke of my experiences at the Australia Council and the ABC where management, faced with cut-backs, had been disinclined to cut itself back while finding it all too easy to hack away at programs. If O.P. wasn't careful he'd finish up with oodles and oodles of arts managers and less and less art.

'But our situation is critical,' says a bloke from the Indian Foreign Service boasting that, effectively, he's running many of India's cultural institutions. 'They're so appallingly managed that we're called in to run them for them. I'm meant to handle the export side of the arts, to send Indian culture out into the world. But I finish up running the organisations.'

One tries to imagine Foreign Affairs in Australia running the arts. Alexander Downer as cultural commisar.

But I don't want to rain on O.P.'s parade. There is, after all, no business executive in Australia like him, someone who's devoting all their efforts, not merely their money, to an artistic crusade. And while he still looks like Buster Keaton and Boris Pasternack I'm now reminded of another sorrowful countenance, that of Don Quixote.

To cheer us up I suggest that India introduce a practice that Australia never got round to implementing: the dazzling notion of paying artists to stop. Any number of Australian filmmakers should have been pensioned off after their first film but, instead, were permitted, even encouraged to make others. Which got progressively worse. I hadn't been entirely facetious in the old days at the Australia Council when suggesting we say, 'Here's a large cheque on condition that you never write another novel, paint another picture, decorate another ceramic.'

While even this anti-program would have been best supervised by artists, peer assessment has come in for rough criticism. But provided you keep churning the advisory boards over, so they can't become too nepotistic, too cliquey, you've a hope. O.P.'s guests remind me that I'm in the land where bureaucracy itself is an art form.

Well, management's certainly not a science. If it was, there wouldn't be so many businesses in ruin. But O.P. is determined to offer management training, professional development and education programs 'to meet the specific needs and requirements of cultural organisations and institutions'. Trouble is, Australia learnt that each art is different and requires an entirely specific approach. The techniques that best encourage writers are wholly inapplicable to filmmakers, for example.

But where O.P. has got things exactly right is in his artists' community, which we visit the next day. He began by surrounding his worthless, arid land with a high and attractive stucco wall. Then came the plantings of trees. Drive through the gates and you'll find yourself in one of the most beautiful spaces in Delhi, where terracotta buildings are guarded by giant terracotta sculptures — of larger-than-life horses, for example, from somewhere in Rajistan. O.P. introduces me to artists from all over the world who are making pottery, painting or writing poems. There's even a young woman from Belgium who's scripting a documentary on one of her country's social problems.

O.P.'s buildings are as elegant as the man himself and have the same blend of the simple and the sophisticated. Just as his homespun khadi would command the respect of Giorgio Armani, his blend of traditional materials with modern architecture is triumphant.

When visiting Paddington O.P. had been intrigued by my collection of antiquities, while far from convinced that such collections were a good idea. He explained that the compulsion to collect was unusual in India for the principal reason that people didn't like to take religious objects out of their context. A statue of an Indian god belonged in a specific place, in a fixed relationship with villagers or devotees. Wrench it from that place and you effectively kill it.

God knows — gods know — that my collection represents many thousands of years of wrenching. On the other hand, few pieces came from a living culture. The gods of ancient Egypt, Rome and Greece, for example, have long since passed their use-by dates. And that was the second point. In India there was little distinction between archaeology and the present. The past lives in India. There is little, if any difference between some unearthed, ancient artifact and what can be found being used in a village today.

To prove it O.P. showed me his own collection, not of relocated deities but of a few thousand utilitarian objects — such as farming implements, cook pots and baskets — that he'd gathered from across the country. It was one of the most extraordinary collections I've ever seen, made all the more extraordinary because the things were, essentially, ordinary: the finest examples of what could be found in the everyday lives of Indians. Thus O.P.'s baskets transcended the basket, the cook pots were the apotheosis of pots, and the tools and implements as elegant as anything by Brancusi. I examined pieces that might have been three, four or five thousand years old — yet most of them had been created — cast, woven, carved, moulded — this century.

When I first introduced O.P. Jain to my colleagues they were suspicious of him. He was too elegant, too dignified, too distinguished, too idealistic. Simply, too good to be true. But soon they realised that he is true to his beliefs and to his culture. Tax deductibility isn't a factor in his generosity. Nor is he particularly pleased by the attention he receives from the artistic, political and diplomatic glitterati. At the end of the day he wants to achieve something particularly Indian, even Gandhian. He wants to home-spin a superior culture. He wants to use simple materials to achieve a noble purpose.

The Television Tycoon

Another row has erupted in Bollywood. It's bad enough that the American cinema is gaining more access and more cultural influence. But now Bollywood is at war with India's cable television station, an industry that increasingly defies the bureaucracy determined to tie its cables in red tape.

It seems that the cable stations are now running pirated versions of major films days before they open in the cinema. The images may be of appalling quality — probably recorded surreptitiously by hand-held cameras at a studio screening. Nonetheless, the telecasts are having a serious effect on box office returns. A few months back Bollywood beat the threat of video theatres showing pirated prints in cubicles. Now this. So alarmed is the industry that actors, technicians and producers are organising one-day strikes and mass rallies in the hope of getting some bureaucratic intervention

In Australia, a cable war has raged between Optus and Telstra, the former stringing its cables through the municipal trees, the latter burying them under the footpath. In India, thousands of would-be cablers were determined to make fortunes from the new medium — and all of them were fighting for access to the lamp posts. As a result we look up at a spaghetti of wiring, a crosshatching that darkens the sky. And we find our way to Malvica Singh's television station by following the spaghetti. The darker the sky, the closer we are to her headquarters, a new building, already dilapidated, in a back street of the city, surrounded by market stalls.

Nemesis to the bureaucracy, Singh is a big girl, dressed in a power sari, with two or three rings for every finger, her Rolex gasping for air amid a few dozen bangles. She's an Indian Rosanne Barr, fleshy and flashy, loud and outrageous. Her staff clearly adore her. She's surrounded by young and very enthusiastic people who call her 'Mother'.

Singh chain smokes, conducts half a dozen simultaneous conversations with acolytes, juggles three phones and is utterly, brutally candid about everything — from the Indian bureaucracy to her parlous financial situation. 'I haven't been able to pay anyone for a couple of weeks. I suppose I'm technically bankrupt. But we're still here. We're still broadcasting. I'm not going to let them beat me.'

She's trying to run a local version of CNN, an Indian news station, in competition with the likes of the BBC, Rupert Murdoch and Ted Turner. But where they seem to enjoy untrammelled freedom, she is blocked at every turn.

Lighting cigarettes far faster than she can smoke them, roaring abuse and encouragement, bad-mouthing government ministers, proffering cups of tea, gesturing proudly at TV monitors, she is at once monstrous and likable. I can't help laughing at her performance — and she enjoys it. She laughs at herself.

'I decided twenty-one years ago to start India's first business magazine. Everyone said to us, "Who the hell's interested in business? And what are businessmen? They're just crooked people. Why would you celebrate them?" But we started with 50,000 *rupees*, which was nothing, even in those days, and crammed typewriters and filing cabinets into my apartment — and launched the magazine which, today, is the leading business magazine in India. It's got a circulation of 120,000 copies but you multiply it by seven, because in India people share magazines. So, really, the readership is hitting a million. Then we started other magazines which have done quite well. And it's from the money generated by the mags that we got into television.

'When the Gulf War happened, we realised that by putting a dish on the roof you could actually pull down a picture. Nobody had ever thought of it or tried to do it before the war happened. But the Government of India didn't want to allow us, and they blocked us through Reserve Bank rules. So we couldn't pay for satellite time or hire.

'Then we realised that there's one country without exchange controls. And that's Nepal. It's an hour away from Delhi, so we used Nepal as an uplink centre. We fly the tapes there every day, to Kathmandu, and uplink from there. India said no, but Nepal said yes. We've got uplink and broadcast permission for twenty-five years from the Nepal Government. Mind you, Nepal isn't an easy place to do business. Governments fall easy and are prone to being bought and sold.

'Anyway, we presented our deal with Nepal to the Finance Minister in Delhi. I said, "You're forcing me to set up a company in the Channel Islands or in the Isle of Man or in Guernsey or somewhere. You're forcing me to make one of my relatives a non-resident Indian. You're asking me to recycle money to do legitimate business from India, for India. I'm not prepared to do that. So are you going to give me permission to pay through the Reserve Bank for transponder hire?" He looked at me aghast. Nobody had spoken like that to a Finance Minister. But he said, "Fill in your forms and we'll clear it."

'Then we went to foreign financial institutions through Jardine Fleming and raised fifteen million for this project. And we signed an agreement with GE who run satellites in America.

They were going to buy a Russian satellite on which we could get four transponders so that we could create a critical mass of channels. Then the cable distributor would have his satellite dish face our satellite. So then everything's all hunky dory and happy. But it turned out to be a dream sequence. Because the Russians were taking GE for a ride.

'And there we were with $15 million and no satellite. And the Russians said to us, "Until Express 6 goes up, why don't you use one transponder we've got, Station R transponder, which is about to start wobbling, but by the time it begins to wobble, we'll have the new satellite." And being sheer innocents we walked into a trap and were stuck on a wobbling satellite. What a waste of $15 million! So we went to the Indian share market to raise another $18 million. But the share market in India collapsed.'

She lights another cigarette and orders more tea.

I sympathise: 'You're not having a good trot, so far.'

'No. I think it's a wonderful trot. Because what I learnt on this trot I wouldn't have learnt in Harvard Business School, that's for sure. So there we were, the market's collapsed in India, we can do nothing. In the meantime I've got a wobbly satellite. I've bought this business. I've put in a studio. I've hired 150 journalists and technicians and VT editors. And because I've only got one channel on the wobbly satellite, I'm forced into omnibus programming. Which is the worst thing you can do. Because you're running away from your focus.'

'An omnibus channel being a general purpose channel? A bit of this, a bit of that?'

'Yep. A little bit of news, one or two bulletins, very little politics, lowest common denominator entertainment. And I hadn't gone into television to do that! But we had no other option. I should have closed down and said, "To hell with it, I'll wait six months." I should have cut my losses and started again. But at that point it would have felt like failure. So I decided to hang in and carry on.

'So we started borrowing money. The interest rate was 18 per cent but some of the money cost between 22 and 35 per cent. A killer! But we saved money by making almost every program in-house. I started running the place very lean and mean. A great learning experience!'

'So there you are, making programs, and transmitting them on a wobbly satellite. Was it wobbling very badly by then?'

'Yes, you couldn't see a thing. So why would anyone want to show us? Or watch us?'

'But the business magazine? Still okay?'

'Cash cow. "Why get into television?" people ask. "You're raking in money in print. Why are you doing this? Why are you having a bigger and bigger hole on your balance sheet?" I'll tell you why. We believed that in a country like India if you're not in television you're making zero impact. Because your magazines address a very limited English-speaking audience. If you want to be a media company you have to be in television. It's not just about leisure, as it is in the West. It's the most important method of accessing information for people in this country who've no access to museums, to libraries. And who have to put up with a third-rate educational system.

'I believed you could make knowledge fun. And irreverent and questioning. That was the premise on which we had built this whole idea. But by this time the people who'd invested all those millions were getting a bit ...'

'A bit wobbly, like the satellite?'

'Exactly. They were saying, "Look, eighteen months have gone by and where are our returns?" And I'd say, "Don't be silly. Eighteen months isn't long. We're not making biscuits or tyres for cars. It takes longer."

'Then the Intelsat, which is a company in Washington, had a satellite over Cyprus. And I managed to persuade them to move that satellite over the Indian Ocean area. Which they did.

'But while I'm fighting City Hall, Murdoch doesn't have to abide by any regulations in this country. Nor do the BBC, which can uplink live, raw footage into its studios in London, cut the film, and show it on BBC World. But I can't uplink from Mumbai to Delhi! And Rupert can make his service look Indian because he has Indian presenters sitting in London.

'But they don't begin to understand this country. God, if I can't understand it, they definitely can't. So they don't bother me.'

'How are you handling the languages?'

'English 50 per cent, Hindi 50 per cent. It's the north–south divide. The south understands English and hates the idea of Hindi, and the north understands Hindi. But the urban Indian understands both languages. They're bilingual.

'Anyway, we've shifted the focus to a news-information channel. And we started doing news on the hour. Up to four months ago we had to send a tape from Mumbai to Delhi on the last flight, which was the news tape for the morning bulletin. So there was someone at the airport collecting all these tapes from all the last flights. And, of course, we get a lot of fog. And our planes don't run on time. But we managed it. And now we have a transponder that we use to send the news on the hour to Singapore. So we're bouncing our programs from Singapore! But it's better than sending tapes. But it's all because of silly bloody government regulations! All this nonsense costs the poor country eight to ten times more than it should.

'The Indian financial institutions don't understand the service sector. They've been bankers to the command economy, to manufacturing and industry. So that's another battle we're trying to fight. To get the bankers to break their mindset. We get no monetary support or investment from the Indian financial institutions. The Western strategic players look at us as someone to piggyback on and make a killing in the last great market left in the world.'

'And what about advertising?'

'We were getting no advertising. And I was constantly being told to do lowest common denominator entertainment stuff to get advertising. Because that's what India wants. I don't buy that! So I went out to the market myself, three months ago, spoke to all the top agencies and said, "This is what I want to do. I want to run a news, information and current affairs channel. I'm not going to do anything else. If you guys feel the corporations are not going to support this kind of endeavour, please tell me, we'll close it down and go back to print." To put it crudely, they've all come around and we started generating advertising revenue. By next year, that's our next financial year, we should break even.'

'And Indian viewers will get Indian news, not news filtered through European television systems?'

'I think they need both. I don't believe in censorship. I think you've got to give people choices and this country's never had any choices. It's been controlled. It's a controlled economy. We haven't had the choice of buying this teacup as opposed to that pot. Let Murdoch come here! It's bloody tough. He's not going to be able to pull it off. He'd be able to pull off an entertainment channel. That's easy. Buy a little bit of flesh here, a little bit of violence there. All human beings like that. But he's not going to be able to pull off news and current affairs. He'll be too concerned about how governments will react to his positions. But I'm not concerned about that. I'm an Indian and I'll react the way I bloody well want.

'If you look at the Star network, it started with a lot of slipshod stuff. With repeats of what Murdoch had shown elsewhere in the world. With stuff that cost him nothing. Now they're making locally based programs, but they're all soaps, serials. What this country needs is the debate, the discourse. For us, for Indians, politics is life entertainment. And we must never forget that. Politics affects our everyday life. It affects whether you can put your switch on and get electricity. We're a very, very difficult polity. People want to know about it. Why do we assume that everyone's foolish?

'This is a society that's 5000 years old, with great philosophies behind it, with lots of influences from all over the world. And it's looking for serious inputs, for serious ideas. And television is the only way to do it! If you can digitise your signal you can have five or six channels on one transponder. You could have Open University channels. You could have language-learning channels. You could have interactive computer channels. You could do a lot of things.

'This is TV One. It stands for TV International. And I call it international because there are no boundaries to television.'

Gita and Gurus

Gita Mehta has charted the course of the West's fascination with India, and India's somewhat cynical response, in *Karma Cola*. Now we sit in a Delhi garden together, she dazzling in white silk and gold sandals, her toenails and talons dripping in crimson enamel, dropping French phrases into her rapid-fire English conversation. ('*Au contraire, mon cher.*') And dropping more names more quickly than anyone I've ever met.

GM: You've just been to the presidential palace. As you know, when they decided to make Delhi the new capital and shift it from Calcutta, they had to build a whole new city. The Delhi that surrounds us is a monument to imperial ambitions. Wherever you turn there's evidence of yet another empire's palaces and forts. And the British had to compete with that imagery. You see the British trying to match the imperialism that India had always had.

India is now witnessing the constant ebb and flow of ever lower definitions of realpolitik as we seek to find the politics necessary to govern one-sixth of the human race, by consensus. We cannot adopt the Westminister model, which is first past the post. We've got too many people, a billion people fighting to go first class.

Gandhi's was an ideological, a sociological, a moral approach. He died before India had to go into the populace politics of democracy. You know, I was on a television program with the American couple, now married, who ran the presidential campaign, the husband for Clinton, the wife for Bush. They call them the Romeo and Juliet of American politics. And they turned to me and said, very graciously, 'It's wonderful that India is a democracy. How interesting Indian elections must be.' And I said, 'Yes, and both of you are genius spin doctors. Tell me, how would you spin an image which includes every voter in Canada, North America, Mexico, eastern Europe and western Europe, most of them illiterate, voting in seventeen different languages for a common government? How would you spin it?' There was a moment of silence then they suddenly understood the scale.

You know, fifteen days ago we finished an election for 600 million voters. And everybody said, 'Nobody's going to come out in this election. This is a mid-term election that didn't need to have been called. They'd just had a general election twenty months ago. They're not going to turn up.' Yet over 60 per cent turned up! That's almost double the turnout of the United States. It's higher than the turnout that voted in Blair. How can I not be optimistic?

PA: You wrote *Karma Cola* almost twenty years ago. It was a devastatingly accurate picture of the West in the middle of what Australians call a cultural cringe, hungry for anything with an Indian brand on it. Most of all, it seems, for fake spirituality.

GM: Oh, the spirituality was false. It was infantile. Instant salvation. Instant enlightenment. Because ours was the baby boom generation of instant gratification. And equally I was trying to show that all Indians wanted was materialism. They wanted the gold Rolls Royces, the gurus wanted the gold toilet seats. We were prepared to exchange anything, including eternity, if we could get some of the toys of the Western world. So it wasn't one-way. It was mutual.

PA: How was the book perceived in India?

GM: Initially no distributor would bring it in. 'Indians don't have a sense of humour,' they argued. But it finally arrived and, to my delight, became the fastest selling book in Indian history. An Indian graphic artist, a young guy, twenty years old, came to me and said, 'You've written a perfect book for Indians. Two-paragraph stories. One sentence, one point.' So Indians loved it. Because what people don't understand, indeed what the Indian distributors don't understand, is that India has a huge sense of humour. There was a great Indian economist who's just become Master of Trinity in England, at Cambridge, and before that held the dual post, the first time ever created, of Philosophy and Economics at Harvard. And he's just given a series of talks to the World Bank. The first talk was titled 'More Playful Than Now'. And what people forget, and what I try to point out in *Karma Cola*, is that Indian philosophy has philosophised the idea of the practical joke and the double entendre.

PA: I find any amount of moral earnestness in India, an abundance of charm and intensity. But what about irony?

GM: Irony is a skill that allows you to distance yourself. Please tell me how it would be possible to survive in India unless you created something of a *cordon sanitare*.

PA: And humour? There seems to be very little humour. In this you, Gita, are different.

GM: Tell me about it! No, I'm not different. But there has been this tradition — I believe it comes out of a colonial mindset — the refusal to be liked! I consider myself to be profoundly post-colonial and there are many like me. The younger generation is even more so. It does not feel the necessity to justify itself and the proof, Phillip, is in the music. These hybrid music forms, and Bangara rock! Indian kids write a song. It is called 'Arranged Marriage' and they make it into a number-one hit in America! Now tell me, how confident do you have to be to take the mickey out of yourself to that degree? I disagree with you. Yes, there is this kind of London School of Economics rush of five-year planning. *Serioso*. We cannot be Indian unless we are extremely stern. But this is totally antithetical to classical Indianism, where our gods, our gurus, our holy men, where *everybody's* cheating everybody else at a rate of knots. You see, our mythology is the only way we take human behaviour and writ it large. In the West you're constrained to only do this through opera, you have no other medium for it. So I believe that the kind of moral earnestness you're talking about comes out of a quasi-colonial mindset where self-justification is all. And where too many people believe they're the voice of God.

PA: Gita, you're an international woman. The 747 is your address. Your husband is one of the most powerful figures in US publishing. So you can see, very clearly, the impact on Indian culture of the great US juggernaut. Do you view it with amusement or equanimity?

GM: I'm not sure that it's been eroded yet. It's really interesting that India is the most heterogeneous country on Earth. Then we've the mass media and mass marketing carrying with it the velocity of global marketing, the power of the homogeneous. Now, I believe that India is today the face of humanity and electronics the face of the machine. If it wins we will be like bricks in the wall, clones of each other, eating the same food, dressing the same way, talking the same talk, admiring the film stars. But India? It may avoid the confrontation. My hope, my prayer (and actually because we're one billion anarchists), my *belief* is that we will take the homogeneity of America and put it through some weird organic process and retain our heterogeneity and make of American homogeneity something which is peculiarly Indian.

PA: You see glimpses of that on the music channels. MTV failed on its initial onslaught in India. Its idioms were hybridised, turned on their head.

GM: Yes! And how about the food. When McDonald's came here they had to change the food! They've had to produce virtual curry burgers! Pizza Parlour comes in — they've got to produce a kind of curried pizza! Yes, you have a paradox. You see kids with a Big Mac in one hand and a cell phone in the other. And here Gandhism is losing out. 'There is something obscene about flashing wealth in a nation of the poor,' he said. Yet that has become our aesthetic. For many in Indian society it's a case of 'If you've got it, flaunt it'. But I have a feeling that it's reaching an apex point, that a repointing of the radar is about to take place. It may not be in Gandhian terms. Because Gandhi was also a kind of Robespierre. His austerity was more than human beings could bear. We need a little room to move. You know, you can eat a little, you can flirt a little — you can do all the things that Gandhi did. But his rhetoric was austerity. And I think that we're going to have a serious discussion about the displays of wealth and ostentation. If you're going to flaunt it, you must, at the same, assist those who are in need.

PA: I don't see much sign of this among the glitterati of, for example, Mumbai.

GM: I do see a beginning of it. I see it very much in the element of the younger generation who work in non-government organisations. I see it strongly reflected in the publishing houses that are coming up. Yes, young people are becoming publishers, bringing into print the nineteenth-century classics of Indian novels! And all of them had a social point of view. And many of them were written by people from the most aristocratic backgrounds. I see it in the extent to which people are working with street children, working in rural welfare. If I could take you round the country, out of Mumbai and Delhi and Madras and Calcutta, to where the non-government organisations are working right in the heart of the most impoverished areas, you'd find kids who have doctorates, you'd find scientists, you'd find them living under the same conditions as the people they're helping.

PA: This is certainly the land of the NGO. They create a sort of political yeast. More, perhaps, than anywhere else in the world. But I hadn't realised that the NGOs were being energised by the children of the affluent.

GM: Yes. People think that all the NGOs in India are foreign hybrids. But the most effective ones come out of here. There's one, for example, run by a swami who was a Harvard scholar, where people adopt all the vows that a priest might adopt. Except that they are secular vows. This organisation is dedicated to freeing bonded labour which, as you know, has to do with terrible debts which may have been incurred by their grandparents and great grandparents. So they must live and work for free for the rest of their lives.

PA: As a child I delighted in playing Snakes and Ladders. Now I learn from your book that it's an Indian game, a game with a very serious purpose.

GM: All Indian games have serious purposes. Chess was about

strategy. Snakes and Ladders like Pilgrim's Progress. You know your virtue will take you up, then you'll meet the slough of despondency. To me, that's an exact parallel of our first five decades as a free nation. We were lucky that our first ladder was provided by the giant who dreamt India. Our second ladder was democracy. Our snakes have been the cupidity, the banality, the opportunism of our political representatives. The deep and millennia-old social justices which we're trying to reverse through consensual means as opposed to dictatorial means. Our ladders are great. Our legal system, our Supreme Court, which is now more and more becoming the guardian of the interests of the Indian people. Some ladders we did get from the British, like the centralisation of an administrative system. Like the idea of a free press. Those nineteenth-century correctives that we took from the British have now been made profoundly Indian. The snakes, equally, are things that we have sometimes taken from the British, things that have created tragedies within the nation.

7

Son of Cochise

George Fernandes looks more like a Red Indian than an Indian and more like the late Jeff Chandler than Jeff Chandler. He's a dead ringer for the dead actor who was, according to the Fantale wrapper, 'easily identifiable by his silvery hair, dimpled chin, muscular physique and distinctive voice'. Mr Chandler, you may recall, specialised in portraying native American chieftains in films such as *Broken Arrow*, *The Battle at Apache Pass* and *Taza, Son of Cochise*.

Despite his Indian credentials George Fernandes is, in fact, a cowboy. Not so much a loose cannon in Indian politics as a loose pair of Colt .45s. His long career has been full of High Noon shoot-outs with, for example, both Coke and IBM.

George likes people to remember that back in 1991 he told IBM executives that they would have to conform to the law of India. They were not impressed and said, 'The last person who made such a request was Charles De Gaulle and we told him we would simply leave France.' So George simply told IBM to leave India. And they did. In the wake of Coke, which had returned to Atlanta, demanding the deposits back on its bottles.

Fernandes is also remembered as the Minister for Railways who has sat on the railway tracks with striking workers, actively encouraging them to attack his own ministry.

There's nothing like a cowboy reputation, combined with matinee idol good looks, to give one a following in politics. At least one Australian prime minister comes to mind, as do a couple of US presidents. While top billing eludes George he's had no difficulty landing plum roles in any government that comes along. Mind you, he's been willing to facilitate matters by finetuning his ideological positions. Thus the firebrand socialist became the President of the Summtta Party which had been flirting with the BJP since 1995. He was poised to share the spoils of office and was making absolutely no apologies about it.

These days Coke and Big Blue are exactly the sorts of companies that Vajpayee wants to welcome to the new, deregulated, all-vibrant, all-stops-out, level-playing field, economically rational political landscape. Yet Fernandes told me he was still opposed to much of the liberalisation that occurred in the 1990s, arguing that it had simply helped the US and multinational corporations to displace Indian labour. He insisted that of the 150 million unemployed in India at least 40 million were well educated; that Delhi's figures proved that liberalisation had created just 8000 new jobs while, in the same period, four million people had lost their old jobs.

'I'm not against economic reform, but it has to be reform that helps most of the country,' he told me, 'and not just two per cent of the elite. And how can a small Indian soft drink company compete with Pepsi and Coke with turnovers in the billions?'

He insists that there's been barely one per cent growth in agriculture and allied services since 1991, and that industrial growth in the 1990s is only half the rate of the 1980s. 'The only areas that have shown growth have been the service sector, the financial sector, telecommunications, hotels and tourism where increases have been as high as 1000 per cent. But the flow of income hasn't helped more than a handful of the urban population.'

And he cited India's textile industry with about twelve million skilled weavers. 'If they're not protected from foreign competition, they'll add to the immense unemployment figures.'

I confess to Fernandes I'm finding it difficult to comprehend Indian politics, because everyone seems to disagree on everything. I'm reminded of being in Tel Aviv where, famously, four Jews equals four political parties. Fernandes is immensely amused and wholeheartedly agrees. 'It's even worse than that,' he says with a happy smile, 'we don't even agree with ourselves. The opinions I express this morning I will renounce this afternoon.'

While his mercurial views and cool dude personality are fascinating, it's Fernandes' appearance that I find most riveting. Those Jeff Chandler looks. As we sit and talk, with Fernandes moving from the laconic to the ironic, from the offhanded to the intense ('I don't give a damn whether I'm in the new ministry or not. Who cares?') I find myself staring at a face that is either the prematurely aged face of a young man or the remarkably youthful face of an old one.

Finally I say, 'George, I want to ask you a personal question.'

He raises an eyebrow. He nods his permission.

'Exactly how old are you?'

He is pleased to be asked. A faint smile plays around a mouth that wouldn't look out of place on the countenance of one of India's dancing divinities.

'How old do you think I am?'

'Well, about fifty.'

The playful smile instantly disappears. He looks stern. No, more than that. He is bitterly disappointed. 'Most people think I look forty,' he says.

I instantly concur with the collective view. 'Yes, you could easily be forty.'

I break another silence by repeating my first question. 'But how old are you?'

He smiles enigmatically. Later I'll check the biographical data and learn that he's either sixty-four or seventy, depending on which birthday you believe.

Behold the Peter Pan of Indian politics. I'm used to meeting gentlemen of considerable antiquity who are in glowing good health, but Fernandes is different. The most Westernised of any Indian we'll meet in the elite, he has got the sort of good looks that cost Californian business executives a fortune — in personal training and cosmetic surgery. So I find myself staring at Fernandes' face for signs of the scalpel. When none can be detected I ask him his secret.

'My urine regime.'

And suddenly I wish I hadn't. George is another Indian

politician whose elixir of youth is his own wee-wee. Moraji Desai (1896–1995) was Prime Minister of India from 1977 to 1979. Founder and leader of the Janata Party, his period as PM was the only interruption to Mrs Indira Gandhi's long period as Prime Minister from 1969 to 1984. Desai was eighty-one when he came to office.

And he attracted worldwide publicity with the revelation that his longevity, both personal and political, was due to his lifetime practice of drinking a glass of his own urine every morning for breakfast.

When asked his view on this practice, Gough Whitlam said, 'Well, I've heard of people getting on the piss early but this is ridiculous.'

Barry Jones recalls any number of questions that Whitlam wanted to ask Desai, such as, 'How do you keep it? In a refrigerator? At room temperature? At blood heat? How do you serve it? With lemon? On the rocks? With a touch of bitters?'

It is perhaps fortunate that Gough didn't raise these issues at CHOGM.

But I wasn't so diplomatic. I couldn't help but point out to George that he is in a position to challenge Coca-Cola for the second time — that he was in possession of a formula that would make Atlanta the Lost City. 'You, sir, have a beverage that could change the drinking habits of the world for the second time in a century.' The formula but not, sadly, the manufacturing capacity.

Here was a challenge for Indian science. Or failing a successful synthetic, perhaps George could, himself, provide the secret ingredient for Indian Coke. After all, everyone kept pointing at McDonald's surrender to the muttonburger as proof of India's success at hybridising foreign influence.

George smiled a moviestar smile. It was then he got the phone call that Mr Vajpayee wanted to see him. A few hours later the President of India would swear him in as Vajpayee's Minister of Defence.

Stop press: Another triumph for Indian bureaucracy and for George's department. The 4th India International Civil and Defence Equipment and Systems Exhibition and Conference turns out to be an exhibition without exhibits. The four-day exhibition ran into rough weather with none of the exhibitors being able to display their wares ... because they'd not been cleared by Customs for reasons that neither the Government of India nor the Ministry of Defence could explain. Exasperated exhibitors who'd spent millions carting their weaponry from across the globe complained of being cheated.

After talking to Fernandes we do the rounds of policy makers and opinion leaders, beginning with Dr Ashock Lahiri, the big cheese for the National Institute of Public Finance and Policy, a former economic adviser to government and an employee of the International Monetary Fund for nine years. He's in the middle of making a TV series on the economic liberalisation of the Indian economy called 'The Elephant Wakes'.

Up until 1991 India was virtually a closed economy, and the country prided itself on being self-reliant and independent. Now, Lahiri believes, domestic deregulation and external liberalisation have led to internal investment. And he denies that the reforms were forced on India by the world's finance institutions. 'No, we'd been talking about doing it for some time.'

Arun Kumara, Associate Professor in the Centre for Economics and Planning at the Jawaharlal Nehru University, passionately disagrees, insisting that, at best, three per cent have benefited from liberalisation while 97 per cent are becoming marginalised by the whole process. He argues that governments are less concerned with issues of unemployment, health, roads and irrigation and far more concerned with issues such as financial flows and capital.

India has been forced to make concessions to foreign companies to attract their investment, says Arun, and this has distracted governments from spending resources on poverty. He sees the states getting less and less money as the federal government pays bribes to the multinationals. To make matters worse, the states are competing with each other and, in every case, the poor are left poorer.

He believes the new BJP government is hopelessly confused about the future. What it seems to be saying is that India should be liberalising internally before it opens itself up to the world, and on that Arun is in agreement. 'India must address under-employment, education and health before we worry about IBM. This isn't easy, especially once you've entered the global market. The big problem is that the big banks and the IMF and other forms of international finance will only help you if you play by their rules. And you only have to look at what happened in Asia to see the dangers, how economies that were in most respects strong can be destabilised by the movement of capital.'

Imtiaz Ahmed is a political scientist and professor at the Centre for Political Studies at Jawaharlal Nehru University, and as a Muslim he's fearful for the future under a BJP government which may, little by little, undermine the notion of India as a secular state. India has always been a diverse and pluralist society, he says, with large numbers of different religions and communities. Thus the constitution enshrines secularism as being central to India's survival. Indeed, the notion of nation is only possible — the diverse communities of India can only be welded together — when space is provided for different communities to function.

He spoke of his fears of the BJP; that it will try to move India towards a uninational, unicommunal nation, defining itself in terms of one prescribed set of core values — Hindu values. And the BJP leadership has made little secret of the fact that it will push to redefine secularism in terms of Hindu values.

On the other hand, he concedes that Hinduism is not one ideology, with one set of clearly defined values or principles. So even any attempt to homogenise Hinduism would be madness. Yet he fears the BJP government will start to talk about modifying the secular nation of the Indian state, which would fuel the fires of Islamic fundamentalism. And when that happens, India will become uncontrollable.

Dr Rajeev Pahargar is a political scientist and a colleague of Imtiaz' at the Nehru University. He concedes there have been problems in the way secularism in India has been working. People are worried that India is moving towards a Turkish or French model, where religion is completely obstructed from the state. Whereas in India secularism has been understood in terms of providing equal preference for different minorities and religious groups. Indian secularism has worked, he says, because it's based on the idea that groups and minorities that are not part of the dominant discourse are inevitably disadvantaged, and therefore it is necessary to provide certain rights that will counter-balance this disadvantage.

Another major element in the debate has been the lack of reform in the Muslim civil code. The Hindu civil code was changed years ago, mainly from pressure from within the Hindu community. Many Hindu leaders were politicised during the struggle against the British and were willing to tackle the issue. But this has not happened in the Muslim community, which is dominated by orthodoxy. At the same time, the Indian constitution gives groups the right to propagate religion, and this has been extrapolated into the right to convert others. So both the Christians and Muslims have attempted to win converts — an alien concept to Hindus who are infuriated to see their young being lured into the other faiths.

Swapan Dasguta, deputy editor of *India Today*, argues that secularism is a non-issue; simply something brought up by the BJP's opponents to try to attract the Muslim vote. To him the key issue is one of attitude. Secularism in India has had a double-standard — the authorities have been insensitive to Hindu needs and wants, while at the same time catering to other religious groups and minorities. Which brings us to the building of the Hindu temple at the disputed site at Ayodhaya, a site also claimed by Muslims. It is the bricks and mortar version of the conflict between the social and the legal codes, between the family laws that exist for Muslims and other minorities and those observed by Hindus.

What of women in politics? I talked to Neerja Chawdhury, the political editor of the *Indian Express* newspaper; to Sabushini Ali, the national secretary of the All India Democratic Women's Association and a former member of Parliament; and to Indira Jaisingh, a supreme court lawyer, about women and politics.

They confirmed that Indira Gandhi did virtually nothing for women's rights in India during her seventeen-year presidency. They mourn the fact that women still vote along party lines, and in some cases sell out on women's issues. For example, it's BJP policy to support reservation for women: 33 per cent of women in Parliament. But one woman MP, Uma Bharti, did a deal with her schedule caste supporters and scotched the legislation.

They agreed that the Indian Women's Movement had been borne out of the freedom struggle; that in many ways the fight for women's rights came less from gender difference than from women's desire to be visible in mainstream politics, to be seen as free and independent. So at a time when Western women were fighting for personal freedoms, Indian women's consciousness was inextricably linked to the national struggle for independence.

Since Independence, the women's movement has had many achievements in a long agenda involving women's health, the practice of self-immolation at a husband's funeral, the problems of infanticide and unequal pay. Nonetheless, women still find it difficult to properly pursue women's issues for fear of being marginalised. It is seen as more important to embrace such overarching issues as casteism.

Yet even in the midst of religious fundamentalism there are signs that women are stirring. Just as Hindi women have worked to change Hindu Personal Law, a growing class of Muslim women is determined to reinterpret the Koran, to find within the texts support for female dignity and independence.

The hour is late for women in India, yet the Women's Movement is in its infancy.

8

Varanasi

Another journey, another train. I'm not cocooned in a quiet compartment, able to snib the door against humanity. I cannot watch the world through the windows. I'm now travelling hard and the only doors are those at the ends of the carriages, the doors that have sealed us all in. There is no air-conditioning. There is no air. The toilets can best be described as off-putting. Once again, reservations mean nothing. People push and shove until I finally surrender a couple of precious inches and allow some people to squash down beside me. 'We're only going as far as Poona.'

I calculate that we'll arrive at Poona at nine at night so there'll still be five or six hours for me to sleep before Varanasi. But after Poona more bare feet clamber over me, intent on occupying even the luggage racks. The train claims to be an express but stops at every other station and hundreds more pile in, usually ticketless, overwhelming the eternally indignant conductors. Yet again it's anarchy versus bureaucracy and, as usual, anarchy wins.

When the train stops it's obvious that, as bad as things are, they could be worse. While I feel like an extra in *Amistad*, the third class carriage on the other side of the platforms has scores sitting on the roof and people hanging their cooking pots and washing out the windows.

The crowds in the corridors are augmented by people selling

cold drinks in ice buckets, or Cadbury's chocolates at an extortionate cost. Now any number of dishes covered in aluminium foil arrive from the next carriage, where they've been cooked by a couple of squatting chefs slaving over an inverted wok.

The train stops again and there's a final, successful assault on my compartment and another family of five manages to fight their way in and sit on the floor and on each other's knees. While everyone proceeds to talk very loudly all night there's no denying that these are charming, delightful people. Once ensconced they help me fight off other invaders, and in return for occupying every inch of space they insist on sharing their food.

The city of Varanasi is the earthly throne of Shiva, the great creator and destroyer. He is on hand to whisper a mantra into the ears of those who succeed in dying here, where pilgrims seek the fourth and most important *Purashartha, Moksha*. This is the Himalayan peak of Hindu belief, which can only be reached by those familiar with the other three *Purasharthas*, or purposes of life: *Darma* (the code of righteousness); *Artha* (the code defining human life in terms of possessions and wealth); and *Karma* (embracing desire and sensual love).

Varanasi's ancient name was Kashi, meaning 'Divine Light'. In the days of the Raj it was known as Banaras. And at long last we're here.

Anaesthetised by exhaustion I stagger from the train, barely feeling my suitcases being removed from numbed fingers by porters. Or, perhaps, by thieves. I'm like Clark Gable and, frankly, don't give a damn. Mr Gable comes to mind because somehow I've wandered into *Gone With The Wind*. This isn't the Varanasi railway station, it's the Atlanta station, as depicted in the Selznick movie. For as far as the dulled, defocused eye can see there are stretchers laid out, the dying and the dead of the Civil War. On closer inspection they are Hindu pilgrims who are sleeping here, waiting for a morning train to Calcutta.

I estimate that there are over a thousand of them — men, women and children — sleeping on the cement. They are, as well, piled up in the vast waiting rooms and are so densely packed on the footpaths that there's no room for my feet. I try to wade through them without stepping on arms, bellies or fingers. In front of me, astonishingly, a woman is trying to navigate a trolley as her luggage is too heavy to lift. And she rolls the chromium casters over hair, clothing, noses. People squirm and scream, then resume their slumbers.

We arrive at the hotel at 3 am. It's in the back streets and rates not a single star. In fact, you would have to go a long way down the cosmic scale until you found something appropriate. Perhaps a minor asteroid or a battered meteorite. On the train it seemed anything would be better. But this? A concentration camp would have a more welcoming reception desk. Yet a miracle occurs. Once we're through the formalities we discover that behind high, galvo gates is a charming garden. With marigolds, daisies and chrysanthemums in bloom. The rooms, though cell-size, are absolutely and utterly clean. And there's an air-conditioning unit that while emphysemic, does cool the air by a couple of degrees. At a point between the door and bed I lose consciousness.

Some time the next day I awake to find myself in one of the cities of the ancient Roman Empire. As surely as the sari recalls the toga, Varanasi recalls Pompeii or Herculaneum, prior to their asphyxiation in the ash of Vesuvius.

While the populations in the ancient world were comparatively small, the population densities, most of all in the walled cities of the Middle East, exceed anything we know in the twentieth century, even the claustrophobias of Hong Kong and Sao Paulo. So when you're pushing through the stinking alleys of Varanasi, trying to avoid the excrement and urine that you hope came from cows, pushing through the herds of them and of people, as you hope you're heading for the vast, sacred sewer of the Ganges, you're back in the back streets of the Eternal City. Trying to find your way to the Tiber.

The city faces east over the Ganges. All the better to salute the dawn in simple, ancient ceremonies. The river is lined with *ghats*, a system of giant stairs and platforms for holy men or funeral fires. Temples, hotels and hospices loom over seventy bathing and cremation *ghats*, casting their shadows on small shrines built around venerable phallic symbols that are as intensely decorated as video arcades or Darrell Lea windows.

Loinclothed men greet the rising sun with marigolds and little paper boats carrying ignited candles. And water is scooped up in brass vessels to be taken back to villages all over India.

The Sardus in their orange robes are there to meditate on *Moksha*, as are the Mumukshus who, close to naked, practise their yoga at the water's edge. Hear the bells, competing with Indo-pop disco music, and smell the incense, competing with the stench of sewage.

It's wrong to think that the ancient world was full of white marble statues and classic columns. First of all, the statues weren't white — they were polychromatic, with painted hair, painted faces, painted eyes and painted fig leaves or painted drapes. Ancient Rome would have looked as lurid as the kiosks selling Catholic kitsch around the Vatican. So Varanasi's exuberant vulgarity, its clash of cultures and colours, is in no way un-Roman. Nor are the tiny shops crowded cheek by jowl, every inch of every way. Here a bloke who's panel beating a motorbike, there someone sells embroidered silks and saris. I remember walking through the narrow lanes of Pompeii looking at the shops where, two millennia ago, bakeries contested with wineries, scribes with brothels.

There's smoke in the air at Varanasi, and drifting ash, but it's not coming from a Vesuvius. The winds are carrying them from the burning *ghats*. Mourners push by, carrying a shrouded corpse on a bamboo stretcher. For Varanasi is as popular with the dying as it is with the tourist and the pilgrim. Just as Mecca is the place to visit for a Muslim, Varanasi is the place to die if you're a Hindu. For if you're fortunate enough to fall from the perch in these ancient precincts, your death is off to a flying start. Hence the hospices looking down on the Ganges where the old and the ailing spend their last hours, or days, waiting their turn.

The Ganges, or Ganga Ma, begins its life high in the Himalayas in Uttar Pradesh and ends its journey in the Bay of Bengal, south of Calcutta. The vast river meanders across an immense flood plain, forever changing its direction. Yet for as long as anyone can remember, the Ganges has remained faithful to Varanasi, gliding obediently along the *ghats* that cluster its banks. Oh, sometimes the river rises 10, 20 metres and engulfs them, filling the lower floors of the palaces and hospices, stealing the neatly piled wood used in the funeral pyres, cleaning, at least at the time, the poisonous mixtures of raw sewage, human and industrial waste, the charred remains of bodies and animal carcasses. But then, very quickly, it resumes its traditional role of spiritual motherhood.

Hollywood has made many films on ancient Rome, most of them ludicrous. There was Louis Calhern as Julius Caesar saying, '*Et tu Brute*' to James Mason's Brutus prior to being mourned by Marlon Brando's Mark Antony; the soundtrack full of the cheers and roars stolen by director Joseph Mankiewicz from the baseball park next to Culver City. There was *Quo Vadis*, wherein all the centurions spoke with big city American accents, all except for Peter Ustinov's Nero. (Ustinov told me it was wholly appropriate for ancient Romans to speak in modern American 'because, after all, the Americans are the Romans of the twentieth century, as powerful and as vulgar'.)

The film that got the ancient world right, not to mention the ancient Romans, was *The Life of Brian*. Too many films on New Testament times had blond, blue-eyed Christs — most notoriously, Tab Hunter crucified with shaven armpits. But *The Life of Brian* gave us the least romanticised of views. There was the sense of the chaos and confusion that characterised the era, as in the long pan over prophets ranting at the crowds along a city wall. Each claimed to be God's messenger, each saw something different in the signs. Varanasi has all of it. Like Rome, it is a city of competing deities where religious conflicts can, at any time, erupt.

And the great buildings that line the Ganges, above the endless and perilously steep steps that descend to the water's edge, remind you of the pre-Christian world because, of course, they belong to it. Here, Christianity, like Islam, is a recent addition to the smorgasbord of faith. The Tibetan monks you see in the street remind you that it was only a few miles from Varanasi that Buddha attained his enlightenment. But the Ganges remains a metaphor for the most ancient of religious cosmologies, the Hindu. All the others are recent arrivals, passing fads.

As you stand on the *ghats* and look at the panorama you're reminded, irresistibly, of Turner's paintings of ancient Carthage. Just as the Hindus' menagerie of gods, its realm of human deities and animals, recalls the vestry of ancient Egypt, as surely as the sacred cows remind you of the bulls of Apis. The only faith that's missing here is Christianity. There is, of course, a story that Christ died in India. Somewhere in this vast country you can visit his grave. But despite the tenure of the British, despite the reverence given to Mother Teresa in Calcutta, Jesus is, at best, just another tourist.

It can take you an hour to go a few kilometres here, an hour spent breathing air that lacerates the lungs and scalds the eyes. The fastest way to travel is to walk and yet few do so. Instead they choose the mode of travel appropriate to their station in life. You can be drawn in rickshaws. You can be peddled in a trishaw. You can be propelled behind a screaming two-stroke, or behind an emaciated horse, or in a car. It makes little difference to the outcome. You'll arrive no sooner or later.

The caste system is seen more vividly in Varanasi than anywhere else in India. At the burning *ghats*, for example, there's even different firewood for various echelons in society, and the burning of the bodies remains a Dalit profession. Foreigners are forbidden to watch the goings-on and regulations ban photography. Yet the river is full of boats jostling for position as tourists aim their zoom lenses. Or, for just a few *rupees*, you can be guided up dark stairways to a vantage point only metres above the pyres where, if you're discreet, you can photograph or film or tape to your heart's content.

As you approach the *ghats* you see members of the deceased's family having their hair cut off by the barbers who crouch in their doorways. You see people buying the appropriate garlands or, perhaps, another brocaded shawl to add to the technicolour shrouding. And then you see the piles of wood, where entire forests have been felled for the cremations. There are cheap logs for the impecunious and wood of such excellence and rarity that it's reserved for the odd tycoon, the prominent politician or movie star. Mr Ram, a Dalit with a gammy leg — he'd toppled down the *ghats* and the broken limb hadn't mended properly — did his best to explain proceedings. He told me that some funeral pyres can costs tens of thousands of US dollars — for the wood alone.

I walk among the piles of wood, watching young blokes splitting them with wedges. The logs have been brought from all over India, on trucks and trains, to be floated down the river to the *ghats*. I watch them building a pyre, little more than the length of a body and not much wider. And around a metre high. I watch a corpse, wrapped as tight and white as a mummy, being lifted from a bamboo stretcher onto the pyre, and it is still in rigor mortis. As Mr Ram explains the subtleties, I see the body being anointed in ghee, something akin to melted butter. 'This will help the body burn, but it will also conceal the smell of burning hair,' he says.

For years Westerners, Dharma Bums, hippies and an endless succession of gurus groupies have come to India wanting to learn how to live. When, in fact, Indian culture is concerned with learning how to die. The ceremonies I watched, the succession of ceremonies, remind me that death at Varanasi, on the banks of the Ganges, was as deeply felt and as formally observed as death in ancient Egypt, along the banks of the Nile.

We're not very good at death in the West. A few weeks before leaving for India I'd attended my mother's funeral in a bland, multi-denominational chapel attached to the crematorium at Springvale. Despite the best efforts of her grand-daughters, who'd chosen the music and carefully written out their tributes, the proceedings were as anti-dramatic as modern undertaking could manage. I remembered the other occasions I'd been in this chapel, or one very like it, while nearest and dearest had been disposed of in proceedings as devoid of emotion, let alone passion, as was inhumanly possible. In Australia we cry at weddings while smiling uncomfortably at funerals, treating death as a mild embarrassment. But here, in India, death is not denied.

'Is everybody burnt?' I asked Mr Ram.

'No, not everybody. Not people who've died of the plague. Because we would breathe in the smoke and die of the plague ourselves. Nor do we burn little babies. As you can see, they are taken out in boats and given to the waters.' And I do see. Three boats are being rowed to the middle of the river, three tiny mummies lowered into the flow.

'There are six kinds of people who we do not burn, who go instead into the water. Children are the first. Then certain holy men, and leper men. And fourth, those who die of snake bite or cobra bite. The fifth kind of people who do not make fire have smallpox. And the sixth are ladies pregnant. And all animals go into the river. Burning is for humans, not animals.

'And why do they put body in the water? Example, children. Children they don't burn before the tenth year. Why don't they burn? Because children body is innocent body. Children speak not lie. Children not kill people. Children not make bad business. So children karma is very good. Children body is natural and pure. Children skin is very soft, like flower. So a child body is a flower body. So nobody like to put flower on the fire. Flower go in the water.

'Suppose your friend give you a flower. You like the smell. You like to put it in the water. But you don't put it in fire. So they put a children body in the water. They tie it with stone and they take a boat and put directly into the river.

'The second people who don't burn are holy men. They spend their life to find the spiritual power to find a god and goddess. So holy men make not a marriage. They make not sex. They don't love gold, silver. They don't stay with a family. They don't want a house. They leave all material things behind. They are wandering whole life to the temple, to the *ashram*, to the forest, for their spiritual power. So when holy men die they don't burn, they put in the river. Why? Because the river is goddess. So holy men, holy river.

'Leper men, why don't they burn? Because leprosy makes them bleeding, scratching in the hand, in the palm, in the feet. And in the blood there is an animal which is called bacteria. So when people die, there is bacteria in the body and in the blood. So when they put on the fire and burn the body, bacteria burn as well. Bacteria make a smoke, so the people, the people near smell the smoke and perhaps they can catch the same sickness. That's why leper men don't burn. They are put in the water. They are tied with stone so body go to the bottom. And at the bottom there is the big fish, the dolphin, that eat them. So there is no chance the body gets rotten.

'Smallpox man? Why they don't burn? Because there is bacteria. So when they put on the fire the bacteria gets in the wind. People can catch it like that.

'Ladies pregnant? Why don't they burn? Because when you burn the lady you burn the flower. Ladies they are burning, but not pregnant. Pregnant lady they put in the water.

'And this is six. Snake bite. Because when the person is bitten by a snake this happen in the countryside. And when it happens the family think this is not real dead. Because when a person is bitten by a snake they lose the sense, but not the soul. When a person is bitten by a snake, the family does not believe this is dead. They go to a man who knows the spiritual mantras, who knows the mantra of the snake. So this holy man, this spiritual man comes and makes a prayer. They chant the mantras. They celebrate. They make a ceremony. And this will finish the poison and make the life again. Yes, it can be possible.

'But it is very hard to find the man who knows the spiritual power. Because he is a wandering person. He has not a house. He has not a fixed place. In that case the family cannot wait a long time because the body gets changed after one day. It makes a smell. So they bring the body here, but we do not burn the body. Because when they burn the body, you have ashes. So they put the body in the water, but without a stone like other bodies. Because when you put a stone, the body goes deep and is finished by the animal fishes.

'So when they bring the body here, they bring tree planks from a big banana tree. And they bind the right arm, the left arm. They bind to the banana tree. And then they put much flowers, coloured, on the neck, on the head, and they write on a piece of plastic, "Dead by Snake" and hang that sign on the head. And then they leave the body on the water, floating. So when the bodies are swimming on the water, when the body go a little further, maybe some spiritual man see it. And the spiritual man reads the notice on the body, "Dead by Snake". So it is duty to make the spiritual to bring the man to life. And when he does he make more strong his own power.

'But if he don't make it, it means he lost his power. But when the holy man find a person, and give him back the life, then they can come back home, because the poison is finished.

'Sometimes, in the country, there is no big river like the Ganga. So they put the snake-bite person in a little river, hanging on the banana tree. And he's bobbing in the water, his face going up and down, up and down. And when he go a long, long time up and down, up and down in the water, then the water clean the poison. Slowly, slowly, the man get his sense. And then he go home and say, "Hello, how are you!"'

I asked Mr Ram whether this miracle occurs very often.

'Yes, this has happened. That's why they put the man on the banana tree and float him.'

Mr Ram then explains the sequence of events for those over the age of ten who aren't holy men, lepers, pregnant women or victims of smallpox or snake bite.

'The first ceremony is when a person die,' he says, 'when person die in the night, they pick their time in the daytime, maybe ten o'clock. So all the people they come at the house. When a man die, they take the butter, they make the massage of the butter, and they clean the body, and they take off the old cloth and they put white cloth, new cloth for the man or red cloth for the ladies.'

And the brocades?

'Red is for ladies because red is the wedding colour, the marriage colour. And white for purity. And they carry the body, four men from the house, and they bring the body here. And all the way from the house they chant the mantras.

'And here they put the body in the water to purify it, into the holy water, and then they keep the body on the earth.

'Then the family go to the office. They give the name and the address, how the person died, all the information, and get permission to burn the body. Otherwise somebody might kill somebody, and burn, and nobody knows. And when they get permission to burn the body, then they buy the wood. One person they buy 200, 250, 100 kilo wood for burning. The wood has been brought a long, long way by trucks. And they stop the trucks by the bridge you see in the distance, because no trucks are allowed in the city. And this is special wood. This is not just any wood. You can cook your food with any wood but this is a special wood to burn the bones.

'Then the family shave the hair. And they put on a white cloth, because white is a funeral colour here. It may be the son. He shaves his hair and he puts on a white cloth and he lights the fire. It is a fire which is kept inside. It is a fire lit by God, not lit by human. Otherwise the body will not get salvation.

'And they put ghee on the firewood for more flame, for faster burning, and they sprinkle a yellow powder on the face, on the body. They sometimes put sandalwood in the chest so that when the hair burns and the skin burns it will smell like wood. If you burn hair in your room you will see a very big smell. But here the whole body burn, the whole hair burn, but it is not a bad smell due to the sandalwood.

'Yes, they put the body on top, and they bring the eternal fire, go to burn the body. But before burning they walk five times around the body, and they light the fire from the feet. And they wait three hours, because one body takes three hours for burning.

'After three hours they take the bones to put in the water. But the chest of the man, and the pelvis of the lady don't burn. They are very strong. So they take them from the fire, throw into the water. And then they take a pot, a clay pot, a best pot, and put it in the water. And this water they put on the fire. When the fire is getting cool, they take the pot on the shoulder, turn their back and throw it behind them. And break the pot. And then they go straight out. They don't look back again.

'Why do they make five rounds before burning? Because that is a sign, a symbol for the fire elements. Because bodies are made by the five elements, so after death all the elements must go back to their own places.

'Why do people bring the body here to burn? Because this is a spiritual place, a very holy place. Because they find here all five elements in one place. First, they put the body in the water for purification. There is the first element. Secondly, they put the body on the earth. That is the second element. Third, they put a fire to burn the body. That is the third element. And air makes more fire, more flame. And that is the fourth element. And the fifth element is the spirit, the soul. You cannot see the soul but you see the smoke. The smoke which is going to heaven for rebirth, for reincarnation.

'The family take a bath in the river after the burning. Then they go back home. When it is an old person who has died, then families are happy because the old man or the old woman has had a long life. So they make a small party, and then they go home. When an old person die they come with music.

'The man who shaved the hair, the husband or oldest son, wears the white cloth for ten days. Ten days. And for ten days they don't touch anybody and nobody touch him. They don't take a meal. They keep fasting for ten days. And every morning they come to the river with rice, sugar, milk, water, flour — all these things. And the Brahmin priest will chant the funeral mantra and the family make the reply.

'And on the tenth day, the last day, all the family come to the river. And on the tenth day all the family shave their hair, and they make a big celebration to the river, a big ceremony to the river. And then they come back home and at the home make their special foods. But this food is not for the family, this is the food for poor men, for beggar men, for holy men. So why is this food for poor man, beggar man, holy man? They are a blessing to the dead body to get better incarnation.

'Then the men take off the white cloth and give it to the poor men and they put on new cloth and go to live the normal life. But sadness is going on for one year, so for one year people are not invited to make a marriage. They do not go to make any festival or any ceremony.

'Old people want to die here, in Varanasi. Because when they die here, they go straight to the Nirvana and go straight to God. So when people are eighty, ninety, one hundred years old, they are coming from all over India and they wait here to die.

'Some people have no family, no house, no money. Nothing. So other people collect donations to buy the wood, to buy things to burn the body. This is good karma.

'When people are alive, they are working hard, making house, buy gold, buy silver, buy car, buy so many material things. But when a person die, what can they carry? Nothing, just the good karma. So people come here to make a good karma.'

I ask Mr Ram whether he and his family are happy in their work.

'I am a Harijan. I am untouchable man. Only Harijan man can burn the body. This is a job belong to this person. This is low caste. Higher caste people they don't burn body. They don't like to earn the money off the dead body.'

I ask about the municipal crematorium with the tall chimney, smoking not far away.

'That is not for Hindu. It is not for people who believe the religion. It is very cheap.'

What about poor Hindus? Do they use the crematorium?

'There is no question for the poor. Hindu people help the poor to do the funeral. They know that two things never stop. When a person die, nobody can stop this one. And when a girl is growing, coming to the age of marriage, nobody can stop. If your daughter, she's become a ten year, she's in love, you cannot stop, nobody can stop this.'

You can't stop love and you can't stop death.

Mr Ram agrees with me. 'This is the truth.'

I see a body being prepared for burning, but the procedure is different. The body is being completely covered in pieces of dung, like a crust of pastry.

'Yes, the cow shit. The cow shit is dry. They cover the body, so make it like a pot. You can't see the body. It more better. It covers the body and there is no need to touch it again. The body get finished in the fire. When they don't cover the body, they have to touch it again and they have to poke at the bones. They have to break the skull. That's why it is better to cover more. But it is expensive.'

In one of the first columns I wrote for a newspaper, over thirty years ago, I recalled the terrors of a four year old lying in bed thinking about death:

Will I know I'm dead? Will I be able to think? Will I have memories? Will I lie there in the grave feeling the slow passing of the endless days or will 100 years seem like a second? Or will it be nothingness? If so, what colour is nothingness? Black or white? I push my face into the pillow and see colours swirling up in the darkness, and I feel myself falling into the night, through the trees and the clouds, beyond the reach of the wartime searchlights, past the moon and the stars, until there's only darkness and a vast emptiness. And still I fall, falling *upwards* in a vast station of terror. Or *mortal* terror. For I realise that eternal space and the eternal time of death are one and the same thing. That both go on and on forever, and neither can have an end.

And yet they must. Nothing can go on without stopping. Everything must have a beginning, an ending. The thought of eternity is so awesome that I feel an orgasmic dread that chills every atom. So I sit up in bed and fumble for the lamp, wincing in its glare and saying over and over to myself, 'I'm Phillip Adams and I live at 798 High Street, East Kew.' Using the light to block out the ultimate darkness and those pitiful pieces of data to protect me from the reality of the abyss.

Time and space curve in on themselves. Science deals with the cosmology not of eternity but of billions of years. And of the major religions, only Hinduism comes close to the scale of the cosmic enterprise. Christianity is crammed, claustrophobic, as is Islam. Buddhism has the sense to shrug the whole thing off. Hinduism alone deals in what science calls deep-time, in more billions of years than the Big Bang provides, and in concepts that, with a bit of a nod and a wink, can be seen as analogous to state-of-the-art theory. At the same time, it confronts the ancient anxieties that I felt as a child, sleeping in the sleep-out, turning fear into faith, panic into ritual.

For half a century I've lived without religious beliefs of any sort, regarding them as the wrong answers to unreasonable questions. But you cannot help but be impressed with the accumulations of belief that accrue to Hinduism, like mussels to an ancient pier. India has made an art out of dying, and Varanasi is its art gallery.

Years ago I found myself at Benares, at Varanasi (the names of Indian cities seem to be in a constant state of flux), on the eve of a lunar eclipse. I was told that it was the first such eclipse in many centuries and, consequently, almost a million village women were expected to come to the Ganges to ablute in its holy waters. And come they did, in their vivid saris; the poorer the woman the brighter the colours. The crowds were like immense flocks of parrots, budgies and lorikeets. Waiting for them, in long lines along the *ghats*, were the beggars in their drab clothes, in dung-coloured *dhotis*, in the plumage of that international opportunist, the sparrow. And each of the visiting parrots, budgies and lorikeets gave each of the sparrows a gift. A single grain of rice. Just one.

But multiply a grain of rice by hundreds of thousands and you have an outpouring of grain, as consequential as the wheat pouring from an Australian silo into a railway truck. The beggars' tiny bowls were soon full to overflowing, as were the cavities of their laps. And I saw them bailing the rice out, piling it up behind their bodies, lest they looked too fortunate. But in a few moments their bowls and their laps were full again.

I watched the spectacle from a boat on the river, while my guide, with the unforgettable name of Mr Gosh ('I did a PhD in beggary at the university') explained to me the cosmology of beggary, its important role in the Hindu scheme of things. The importance of giving and receiving.

Each person had been given something; a tiny something. This is beggary as a cosmology, as a theology, as some sort of metaphor for the mystery of being. Here the beggar is a spoke on the wheel of life. I cannot begin to comprehend the theology but it is powerful.

Varanasi will soon have two million people, living and dying within its precincts. That's before you count the pilgrims and the tourists who come in their millions. And the sewage pipes for all drain directly into the river. There are places where you see the water burning, where the sewage turns into methane and ignites.

So the river that heals is increasingly the river that kills. The Central Government in New Delhi has spent hundreds of millions of dollars building high-tech waste plants long the Ganges — facilities that are wholly inappropriate. For a start they depend on electricity so when the power fails as it does frequently in Indian cities, they stop operating. And they're overwhelmed during the monsoon season and simply shut down. At the best of times they're too expensive and the cities cannot afford to maintain them.

The results are streets awash with sewage. Local residents were so angry, a while back, that they forced a city water engineer to stand for hours in a pool of shit and urine to give him a better understanding of the problems of toilets backing up into their homes and streets. Now a new campaign is attracting international attention.

The Ganges gives so much, receives too much. This is why I met Veer Bhadra Mishra, in his own personal temple above his own personal *ghat*. He is the head of the Sankat Mochan Temple, one of the principal temples of this 3000-year-old city. And this man of the spirit is also a man of science, Professor of Hydraulic Engineering at Benares Hindu University.

Veer Bhadra Mishra is spiritual heir to the Hindu saint, Tulsi Das who, 400 years ago, wrote a famous Hindi version of the *Ramayana*, one of the sacred texts of Hinduism, first written in Sanskrit. The original manuscript survives in this house, as do a pair of the saint's wooden sandals. Mishra, as he asked me to call him, is a *mahant*, a position that has passed from father to son for endless generations, and he is regarded as semi-divine.

Like Mr Ram, the Dalit who talked to me at the burning *ghat*, Mishra has fallen down the great steps and broken a leg. Months later, movement is still difficult. But he compensates by the mobility of his expressions. He receives me in what Western friends laughingly call his 'throne room' where mattresses scattered on the floor give us a place to sit. He wears his usual light-blue *dhoti* and looks as elegant as any Armani model.

His *ghat* is at the far south end of Varanasi. There are pagoda-like *ghats*, fortress-like *ghats*, old earth-coloured stone *ghats* and modern concrete *ghats* painted in strident colours. There are *ghats* where herds of water buffalo cool off in the water, where washer women rinse out their laundry. And there's his *ghat*, which is painted pale blue, a place where the quietness is emphasised by the chatter of a couple of monkeys and the drone of a sitar.

Mishra is exactly my age. He was made a *mahant* at the age of fourteen. 'Because of tradition,' he said, 'even the old would come and touch my feet to pay respect.'

But then the *mahant* became a scientist and now the scientist is a political activist.

'A meaning has been given to my religious background, and to my scientific background. Life is like a stream. One bank is for Vedas and the other is the contemporary world, science and technology. If both banks are not firm, the water will scatter. If both are firm, the river will run its course.'

He enters that river five times a day. 'I cannot live without this river. She is goddess, mother, I respect and love her. So the first thing I do in the morning is go to her, take holy dips, and then after prayers I go to the university and I start teaching water resource engineering, hydrology, flood mechanics and such subjects.

'I know what is pollution. I know what is fecal coliform and what the dangers are. So I suffer inside, and there is a pain inside which cannot be described in words. And it's because of the suffering and pain that our campaign began. I cannot stop from going to my mother when she needs my help most. A lot of garbage and sewage has been dumped over her body. It is very painful. So you are right to say that I am living with paradoxes. But the Clean Ganges campaign has become the most important thing in my life.'

Mishra's scientific background makes him painfully aware that the fecal coliform count has been known to reach 170 million bacterial per 100 millilitres of water; no less than 340,000 times the acceptable level of 500 per 100 millilitres. This isn't surprising when you realise that 40,000 funerals are performed on the banks of the Ganges each year. In addition, another 3000 corpses, people too poor to afford a funeral, are tossed into the river each year along with around 9000 cattle. And that's only the beginning of what this river must bear. For 500 million people, one out of every twelve in the world, now live on or around the Ganges. One hundred and fourteen cities dump their sewage directly into its waters — waters which begin the flow in an ice cave in the Himalayas, prior to flowing 2400 kilometres through India and Bangladesh to relieve itself in the Bay of Bengal, at Calcutta.

Hepatitis, dysentery, typhoid, cholera kill two million Indian kids each year. And much of it comes from the river. Twenty-nine thousand turtles were released in Varanasi a while back, in the hope that they'd munch on the decomposing body parts. It didn't work. The people ate the turtles.

Mishra wants to see the river protected by a series of natural algae ponds, where waste would be decomposed naturally through a combination of microbial fermentation and photosynthesis. Such algae are the largest single source of the atmospheric oxygen we breathe, and the process would sustain a rich aquatic life, and make fish farming possible. He insists that his plants would be far cheaper than mechanical plants and clean waste water more thoroughly.

The first ponds would be very deep, creating dark sunless depths without oxygen. Here aerobic bacteria would decompose the heavier waste. The second group would be shallower, exposing water to sunlight, thus encouraging algae to grow through photosynthesis which, in turn, would kill off the harmful bacteria. The third ponds would be, once again, deep and still. Here the algae would settle and could be scooped out to feed pigs or chooks, or left there for fish farming. And finally the water would flow into larger dams and could be used for irrigation.

Do the media help in your campaign?

'This is our big strength. But there comes a point when the media shake with fear. I gave *India Today* all the information. The journalist sat here in this room. I've shown him the hand-pumps, shown him the septic condition of the Ganga water downstream from the city. He promised to publish everything. But he did not. And if *India Today* will not publish, then I don't know who in this country will.

'So I have stopped giving interviews. Yet I am an optimist. And I hope that in my lifetime we'll be able to stop the flow of sewage into religious bathing area of Varanasi. At least there. That we will present a model which will inspire the people of India and maybe people of the world.

I remind him of the world's interest in Venice. An international committee tried to save the city. Great amounts of money were raised and sent to Italy, only to be lost to the bureaucracy and corruption.

'The city should have a proper sewerage system. It would be a simple thing to do. We have demonstrated how to do it. We have a feasibility report. I have worked with Oswald Green, Professor of the University of California at Berkeley. He has helped us design a system. We have proposed an advanced integrated waste water pond system. We know where to make the ponds. We will provide jobs in growing fish. This alternative is good. It is scientifically viable. The government must accept it.'

He now has, in principle, the support of New Delhi and the local government of Varanasi. The final obstacle to the trial project for the ponds lies with the state government of Uttar Pradash.

'The effort is welcomed by one and all in India. I think about $40 million has been spent in sewage treatment, in renovating the river face, in providing cheap public toilets and other things. When such a huge amount of money was found, the situation became different. Everybody started fighting each other to take charge of the money, and finally everything gravitated into the hands of the bureaucracy. So the Ganga Action Plan became a bureaucratic program without people's participation.

'We are invited to meetings in Delhi. I go by buying my own train fare with my own money. Yet when the District Magistrates and Commissioner of this place are invited to Delhi to attend the same meeting, they are flown to Delhi by government money. We get no assistance from the government. And I am forced to say that the plan has not succeeded. It has failed to intercept and divert the sewerage. It has failed to treat the sewage properly. It does not control the fecal coliform. The activated sludge plant chosen for Benares was not the right system.

'We must get popular support. People living nearby have given 6000 signatures.

'The government says it is working. They have six professors from very important organisations, from universities and research organisations of the country to certify that things are satisfactory. They are not.

'I am one professor versus six professors. I know that it isn't working. The whole society of Benares knows it isn't working. Look at the bubbling grey water, the stinking water, and you see the condition of the river at the downstream end of the city.'

Does not the Indian Constitution specify the responsibility of providing good water and sewage for the population?

'Yes, there is a water pollution control act of our state government. There is a water pollution control act of our central government. But these acts are irrelevant.'

What about the epidemiologists? What about the medical profession? Are they not your natural allies?

'My son is an MD in general medicine. He works in a village downstream of the sewage treatment plant. The so-called treated sewage flows through that village. Talk of any water disease and it is there — scabies, jaundice, typhoid, dysentery, outbreaks of cholera — the whole area stinks. And the aquifer is polluted. There are hand-pumps to give the villagers water. Black water comes out of them. Water that stinks. There are flies, there are mosquitoes.

'The Ganga is such an important entity in the world that the United Nations should be interested. A hundred thousand people a day come to this city. Almost everybody is having some kind of dysentery. We offer prayers to the divine form of our mother to whom both the demons and the gods come, to touch our lotus feet. She is the provider of happiness and salvation to all of us according to our desire.

'What has happened to this place? Some say that Varanasi is the oldest living city in the world. Some people say it is not the oldest but the second oldest. I say, alright maybe it's the second oldest lived city in the world. Certainly Varanasi is one of the oldest continuously occupied cities in the world. It is as old as the dynasties of Egypt or Mesopotamia. No one sacrifices to Ra or to Bal any more, but 60,000 devotees a day take the holy dip at Varanasi. Or light fires along the shores of the Ganges to Lord Shiva.'

Can the Hindu culture survive? In responding to this question, the scientist and spiritual leader becomes, suddenly, somewhat strident. Though more restrained than the activists of the BJP he, too, sees the Hindu majority as being marginalised by the Islamic minority.

'We must consider these people an endangered species. Well, if birds can be protected, if plants can be saved, let this species of people be saved by saving their holy water.

'The same gods are living with us, the same tradition. I have met many people from Africa at Rio in 1992, at the Global Environmental Conference. In Africa their names have changed, their eating habits have changed, their faith has changed. And because of that change in lifestyle, they need much more money to live. But we have sustained all this for thousands of years. But in the last twenty years, with the television and the market force, with the arrival of the multinationals, I doubt that we will be able to cope with the pressure.

'I shake from within. People do not realise how powerful these market forces and multinationals are. In the next century the multinationals will own the world. I read here and there that governments have to learn to live with them. For the Hindus it's a big challenge. And there is no organisation which is caring for the Hindu society, which works for the Hindu society. Hindus need to orient themselves, to organise themselves so that they can live in the present day world. During the Mogul period, and the Muslim invasion, they cut themselves off from power. They separated, dissociated themselves from power. But you cannot do that any longer.'

Are you saying that the multinational corporation is a more powerful invasion than the Muslims? Than the British?

'Yes, you're giving words to my meaning. Yes. It is more powerful. And if the other side is so powerful, we have to organise ourselves. Who is organising the *sadhus*, the saints, the temples, the monasteries? Hindus are just enjoying their life and earning money. That is all Hindu society is today.'

The Sankat Mochan Foundation is the first group in Varanasi to be on e-mail. Mishra's campaigning is becoming more and more determined. So when he's not dipping in the river, or saying his prayers, he surfs the Net.

On the leg from Varanasi to Calcutta I find myself alone in regal splendour. I have a compartment to myself. A sleeper! With a hand basin! And a reading light that works! My cup runneth over.

Unbeknown to me, my colleagues are not so fortunate. They are sharing the compartment specified on their tickets but, despite chorusing 'Like a tree that's standing by the water, we shall not be moved', they are, yet again, invaded by a madding crowd that, having been revived by the sacred waters of the Ganges, is immensely insistent and energetic. The adage that possession is nine-tenths of the law might work for Australian pastoralists in their tussles over Mabo and Wik but it doesn't count in an Indian railway carriage. There is an escalation of railway bureaucrats, increasingly senior and pompous, their voices becoming increasingly high pitched and shrill.

You can't help noticing, over the years, that in every culture, arrogance and pomposity are inversely proportional to real status; within the lower echelons of management you'll find the most supercilious and domineering personalities. Given their conduct you'd swear that the gentlemen managing this train trip are admirals, generals or High Court judges.

Hearing the racket I emerge from my compartment claiming

to be an immensely important foreign visitor who is outraged by the abuse of my colleagues — a member of Parliament, a diplomat, a close friend of the new Prime Minister. None of this makes the slightest impression on either the officials or the usurpers. I then announce that at least one of the women is my wife. This strategy backfires and soon the four of us are in my compartment while the exultant pilgrims throw a party.

The trouble for the women is that they're women. Everyone we speak to in the religious business, irrespective of faith, tells us the same thing — that the sexes are entirely equal, except for women. Particularly when they're in menses, when they're unclean. And when they say unclean, they say it somewhat apologetically. 'We are talking ritualistically impure, not biologically dirty.' Consequently women are not to be the equal of men in the temple, the synagogue, the church. And it is painfully obvious that they are not to be equal in the railway carriage. In these places, women are to be obedient. Thus speaketh the ancient, deep misogyny that makes men fearful of women's bodies and their mysteries.

We stop at a station where people, sitting in the token shade of a denuded tree, look uncannily like Aborigines you might encounter at Maningrida, in Arnhem Land. Not simply because of the darkness of their skin, but because of the shape of noses, lips, cheeks. And also because of the quality of stillness, of observation. And they have dogs around them, dogs that look like dingoes.

Could there be a link between Australia's Indigenous people and the ancient tribes of India?

People climb onto the train according to their station in life. It's believed that the Hindu caste system originated in the physical differences between the conquering Aryans and the conquered Dravidians. The top three caste levels or *varna* — Brahmin, Ksatriya and Vaisya — were probably recruited from the ranks of the Aryans. Whereas the fourth caste, the Sudra, as well as the Dalits, who fall outside the scope of the four varna, were originally composed of Dravidians. The word *varna* means colour and in the Hindu culture, the colour dualism of white and black has the same association with good and evil as it does in the Judaeo-Christian tradition.

9

Calcutta

If Varanasi gives us a glimpse of ancient Rome, Calcutta resembles Ridley Scott's vision of a future Los Angeles where the street lights and neons are diffused by a pollution that corrodes the lungs and sets you weeping. In Scott's prophecy everyone is on the make, on the take, in a city where crime and commerce have become indistinguishable from each other. In Scott's city, the transport systems of the future glide through the fug while, below them, men pull rickshaws, through drenching acid rain that comes from an atmosphere warmed by exhausts, neons and giant TV screens.

Take away the high-tech and you have Calcutta. Rickshaws on the ground, Boeings circling the airport, drenching rain, the endless hustle, the sense of dislocated time as tradition is confronted by technology. The world now has many cities like Calcutta, with impossible populations, impossible problems. And impassable roads.

The dynamics of traffic are fascinating. We are kidnapped at the railway station by a bloke who pimps for cars instead of prostitutes. He's sleazy, fast-talking, menacing, mendacious. We're shoved into a couple of grotesque, 1950s-style American cars. Too exhausted to argue, we watch as our luggage is fed into the maws between the tailfins — and will realise, the next day, that much of the equipment has been stolen. And aiming streams of vituperation at his drivers, we're directed into the traffic flow. The flow that doesn't. The flow that moves, at best, at walking pace. So that the journey from the station to the hotel, a distance of perhaps 6 kilometres, will take over an hour.

Throughout India the dynamics of traffic are fascinating. The only time the entire system grinds to a halt is when a policeman, or a set of traffic lights, attempts to impose order on anarchy. Left to itself, and most of the time officialdom has abandoned all hope, people simply shove, push and squeeze their way. This is the world of the threat, the bluff, the suicidal lunge.

Years ago I stood in a factory in Warrnambool in Victoria, watching the application of space-age technology to the cutting of cloth. David Jones, the son of the founder of Fletcher Jones, a company fighting for survival, was demonstrating the new technologies that would eliminate any waste of cloth. The component pieces for trousers, suits, jackets, shapes on a computer screen, were jiggled and jigsawed until unprecedented levels of efficiency were achieved — up to 90 per cent.

It's the same with Calcutta's traffic. No part of the roadway is wasted. Almost every inch of asphalt is occupied. By totally ignoring rules and regulations, the ever-increasing traffic consumes every morsel of macadam. Trucks, cars, trishaws, rickshaws are in an endless demarcation dispute that lasts all day and most of the night. It's as if the whole system was driven not by petrol or diesel or pedalling or pulling at shafts but by the sounds of horns on vehicles or bells on rickshaws. The chiming, the honking and the hooting become the motive power that propels as well as compels, compressing the mess of vehicles into a solid mass that might move slowly but, nonetheless, *moves*.

It probably wouldn't matter if you broke down in the Calcutta traffic because, like the moraine on a glacier, you'd be carried along by the incalculable force of the system. It's hard to believe the most sophisticated computer, or the most brilliant programmers from NASA, could improve the efficiency of this immense inefficiency. Even the giant boulevards of the Raj are as full of traffic as the river is of water.

The traffic may inch along, but at least it inches. Given an opening of a few yards a dozen vehicles will instantly contest it. In Calcutta, the driver abhors a vacant space like nature a vacuum. Yet for all the racket, for all the fumes, for all the frustrations of the process, there's a remarkable good-heartedness about it all. Road rage seems as rare as collisions which, when they occur, involve velocities unlikely to injure. What Australians regard as a traffic jam would probably produce agoraphobia in a Calcuttan, be seen as a preposterous waste of space and opportunity. It's like watching a few million years of evolution recorded in stop motion, as the various life forms fight for their niche, their specific habitat.

And here is the most powerful of Indian paradoxes. On the one hand, the Indian people have a placid, fatalistic view of life and death, with the dominant religion having a deep sense of 'deep time'. Yet for all their surrender to the majesty of the millennia, for all the social irony about the futility of ambition, they also have a furious, frenetic, frenzied attitude to existence, with every second as occupied with effort as every inch of road space. Once again, the metaphor of the glacier seems appropriate here. It might take 100,000 years for a great river of ice to grind down the valley, but at the end, at the edge where the ice melts, there are boiling rapids.

Lead-free petrol is as elusive here as lead-free air. The poor blokes pedalling the trishaws, or pulling the rickshaws, must breathe deeply to do the job. The air that fills their lungs is so full of lead from the petrol that when they go to their early graves they'll weigh heavily in their coffins. Or the lead will flow from them, melting from their corpses on the *ghats*.

A quarter of the whole West Bengal population is crowded into 100 square kilometres and the growing population drinks industrial effluent and breathes industrial exhausts. There are 11,576 factories in the heart of Calcutta and forty of these are lead factories. Dr Depuka Chakrobordi, the director of the Centre for Environmental Studies at the Jadaupor University, tells me that there are umpteen incidents involving companies discharging lead into the atmosphere and arsenic into the water table. The pollution caused by industry and vehicles is bad enough, but the problem spirals out of control because of poverty — the majority of the population cooking food on coal stoves.

The professor believes that Calcutta's only salvation lies in building a series of satellite towns north, south, east and west, and then building a huge wall around the original city. 'You could then invite people from around the world to come and see what happens to a city when it ignores environmental concerns.'

As good looking as an Indian movie star, with serious hair, Chakrobordi was part of the Indian diapora. 'I did my PhD in 1974, left India and until 1988 was abroad in many countries. Then I came back and saw the arsenic problem. I could show you a place where 7000 people were affected by drinking arsenic-contaminated water.

'When I told the factory "You are responsible," they said, "We're not responsible." Then I asked the government, "Are you going to do anything about it?" The government said, "We don't know anything about it." So I got inside the factory, like a thief in the night, at midnight. And we collected samples and we analysed and made reports.

'I could take you to places where there are schools beside lead factories, the chimneys' effluent filling the air, the lungs of the students. When it's particularly bad they say, "Okay, you have a holiday today."

'The air of Calcutta is full of lead particles and other sulphur dioxides. It's terrible. I formed my group, and my group began taking measurements, samples, doing analyses.'

Now Chakrobordi is an alchemist who tries to turn lead and arsenic into political activism.

'Our fruitsellers, our hawkers, are breathing in carcinogenic hydrocarbons. The cancer figures will be astronomical. I say, "Hey guy, if you sit there for fifteen years you will get cancer." And he laughs at me. He says, "Hey, mind your own business." Because to him, pollution is nothing. To him, hunger is everything.

'I go to the factories and tell the workers of the dangers. And what do the workers tell me? "Sir, if we die we do not mind. But if you close the factory I will not get a salary, then all my family will die." You must realise that hunger is all-important. Even teenagers' love is nothing when you are really hungry.'

I talk of the improvements I've observed since my last trip to the city. Miraculously, the streets seem cleaner. For all its immensity and intensity, Calcutta is now tidier, in contrast to Mumbai and even Delhi. How has that been achieved? Has he had an influence?

'For the last ten years I am telling what's really happening. Every week there is an article, every month an article. And in those articles you will see that I have a dream. In an article I wrote: "If an angel comes and asks of me what do you want, I will say I have only one dream. Let me take these Calcutta people on my arms so that I can carry them away where they can breathe." That article came out in *Statesman*, one of our leading journals. So slowly people are realising that we're going, we're sinking. We're sinking.

'That's why I want to build small satellite towns surrounding Calcutta, with better roads and conditions. And I want to begin by taking the government offices there away first. That would release the pressure on Calcutta.'

As the formidable Annabelle Quince never takes No for an answer, she spends the best part a week negotiating for a meeting with the Chief Minister Jyoti Basu who, at eighty-four, is the longest-serving communist leader in the world. He became Chief Minister of West Bengal in 1977 and has been there ever since.

While waiting to get approval from Jyoti Basu's office, I walk the streets. The heavy industries are getting heavier, but the tiny factories abound. In every second shop there's a little bloke using a lathe to make unofficial spare parts for cars, bikes, electric fans. Nobody, it seems, buys the approved ones. And nothing is thrown away. Here is a land where you can still get a watch repaired, or shoes resoled. Here keys are cut, and cut by eye, with simple tools, not on a whirling replicator. It isn't so far away, after all, where Afghan villagers are making sophisticated weapons in blacksmith shops.

Calcutta has suffered a calamitous decline since its days at the head of the British Raj and, later, as India's industrial heart. Now the streets are full of people struggling to eke out a living amid the battered relics of its former glory. The State has made considerable advances in agriculture but is struggling with obsolete technology and overstaffing in public sector industry, and with crumbling infrastructure. It has long been notorious among Indian states for its history of bitter three-way confrontations between government, business and labour.

But the government of Mr Jyoti Basu, in office for twenty-two years, has shown a remarkable ability to change its mind. By singing a new song, Basu has managed to attract vast amounts of internal and external capital. So much so that real estate prices in Calcutta, an unfailing thermometer of economic energies, have doubled and redoubled.

Calcutta is the natural hub for eastern India, boasting great reserves of iron ore and coal as well as being a large producer of food grains, tea, vegetables and fruit. Engineering industries abound, including iron and steel, petrochemicals, electronics, software, aquaculture and leather. But the two industries upon which the government has placed emphasis, agro-processing and jute, seem to be in trouble.

At 10.30 every morning the patriarch of the Indian Left leaves his home on the outskirts of town and his convoy of eight cars comes bullying its way through the Calcutta traffic — the parting of which is a miracle comparable to what Moses managed with the Red Sea. Though threatened by the party's 'young fogeys' and increasingly inclined to talk about retirement, Basu remains firmly in control of India's largest and most populous state.

To the late Indira Gandhi, Basu was more of a mentor than a threat. Called Basuji at official meetings, he was 'Uncle' in private. And despite the ideological differences, senior members of Congress, such as the former Prime Minister, P.V. Narasimha Rau, frequently confided in him.

And why not? It would be hard to find a more experienced and cunning politician. He had led a centre left coalition in the 1960s and an all shades of red coalition since 1997. The prime ministership was within his grasp when the Central Committee of his party gave it the thumbs down by 35 votes to 20.

Basu has been the cohesive force in sustaining a coalition government for two decades. In that time he has been a dazzling pragmatist and anything but an ivory tower leader. Ideological constraints, for example, haven't prevented him courting foreign investors for help with Calcutta's notorious power industry. Calcutta was forever being plunged into darkness where now West Bengal can export power to neighbouring states. And he's managed to control the bloody separatist movement in the Darjeeling hills.

Journalists talk of a man who 'keeps his political antennae

tuned to the times'. He's moved away from his earlier focus on land reforms — which have to be among the most extensive and successful in India — to focus his energies on industrialisation and the seduction of private investors. Little wonder that the old communist has become the darling of the corporate world.

Finally we get the nod. No, he won't see us in his office in the city. We're to visit him at his home. It would make sense to add ourselves to his evening caravan so we can be drawn through the traffic in his wake. But failing to synchronise, it takes us ninety minutes to make a trip that should take ten.

Basu lives in an elegant suburb of low-rise apartments where the streets are softened by eucalypts. It's the dream of the middle-ranking bureaucrats to get one of these apartments, which are allocated by lottery. Basu, of course, has done better. He had the winning ticket for Indira Gandhi's mansion, a modernist number that looks vaguely familiar. Finally I realise that it's like the house in Jacques Tati's *Mon Oncle*, the one with the fountain that was turned on when visitors arrived.

As ever, there's any amount of security. As ever, it's half-hearted. What makes Basu's bodyguards different is that they're remarkably friendly, so much so that, when we leave, they stand on the footpath waving. They were still waving as we turned a distant corner.

The television at the hotel where we were staying could, from time to time, be persuaded to yield some sound without a picture, or a picture without sound. That morning it had been in wireless mode and vouchsafed the following information:

> In the first strike against a high ranking politician, Tripura Health Minister Bimal Sinha and his younger brother Bidyut were today shot dead by militants of the banned National Liberal Front of Tripura [NLFT] when they were going to negotiate the release of their third brother from militants' captivity.

When Basu enters the little room where we have set up the microphones — a bleak, white room decorated with kitsch collected on his travels, or brought to him by visiting delegations (Japanese dolls, African carvings, a chromium-plated Eiffel Tower) — he is grieving over the death of Minister Sinha, an old friend and comrade. Tripura is another of the communist states, so tiny as to be forgotten. 'There are a lot of terrorists in such a small state,' observes Basu.

Like the President in Delhi, he is another glowing, immaculate old bloke. Looking more like a holy man than a hit man. Someone who knows where all the bodies are buried. Odd that a life in the rough and tumble of politics seems scarcely to have touched him. We're used to watching prime ministers age decades in the few years they spend at the Lodge — Fraser, Hawke, even Keating — emerging from the experience looking like their own fathers. But Basu is ageless. Externally, at least, he is unscathed.

Anthony Benn insists that there are, essentially, just three types of politicians: the maddies, the fixers and the straight men. Fixers, of course, abound. Bob Hawke was a fixer; Neville Wran was a fixer; Graham Richardson was a fixer — indeed, he's the exemplar of the category. The straight men come in droves: Cain, Bannon, Greiner, Fraser, Beazley. In England, on Benn's turf, the straightest of straight men would be John Major. But it's the maddies who, invariably, are the movers and shakers, the people who for good or ill change things. In Australia their numbers include Keating, Kennett and, yes, Bjelke Petersen, whose careers are analogous with those of international maddies such as Thatcher and Reagan. In Indian terms Mahatma Gandhi was a maddie, Indira Gandhi a fixer and Rajiv Gandhi a straight man.

What category is appropriate for Jyoti Basu? Is he straight? A fixer? There's certainly not a trace of the maddie in this urbane, subtle man.

I asked him why communism has not been more successful across India, given that Bengal and Kerala, particularly Kerala, the Scandinavia of India, have done so well.

'That is the question we ask ourselves. But we are not yet able to find the answer. Many of the freedom fighters who struggled against the British spent long years in prison. Of those who continued in politics, most came to our party which helped us both in the countryside and among the worker middle classes. It culminated in an ideology that people accepted. They realised that we were serious people, fighting for their interest. In the beginning, we led the great peasant struggles for land. Since then we have lost much influence. But this question will be the most important question at our party conference, which we've had to postpone because of the parliamentary elections. We will try to find an answer.'

I tell him that I've put the same question to people across India, to newspaper editors, to members of the new BJP ministry, to academics and analysts, and they all say that communism is unimportant in India, that communism is finished. Indeed, they argue that the left is now irrelevant. How can this be true when there are such great social problems to be dealt with?

'Actually the left is the main force in the opposition in Parliament. And we remain powerful in Kerala and in West Bengal. So we are not quite finished yet.'

We talk of the communist split in India in the 1960s, of the time when Basu split with Moscow. 'Are you, a man of eighty-four, still in the process of political evolution? Are you still modifying or changing your views with the passing of time?'

'Our strategy is that we want a people's government, a government of the left, and later on, socialism, communism, and all of that. I still believe this, that we can change man. But tactics are different. They change from time to time according to the situation. And you are right about the past, we were guided by the Soviet Union. Later we got friendly with the Chinese party as well. But they went against us. We came into government for a little while in 1967, a sort of a coalition government with a group who'd broken from the main Congress Party. And the Chinese party, in the middle of a cultural revolution, whatever that meant, attacked us. Why were we in the government, a bourgeois government? That sort of thing. And so they fell out with us. So we kept our cool. We did not attack them. We carried on. But we only lasted a little while, about twenty-two months. And twice we had elections.

'Later, we got friendly with the Chinese again. They invited us to Beijing. And I asked them, "Why did you attack us, from Chinese radio?" And they said, "Why do you want to discuss this? Many of us were in prison at that time. China made serious mistakes." So that is that.

'But we have come to the conclusion when we formed the Communist Party of India, Marxist, in 1964, that we must not be guided by any other party, however strong, however big. We must be guided by ourselves.'

PA: Well where are you guiding yourselves now? For example, you're encouraging outside investment into Bengal. Will you be able to tolerate the process of privatisation that is sweeping the social democracies?

JB: You see, we are a part of India. We are not the Republic of West Bengal. So policies, particularly industrial policies, are decided by the central government. We have to go along with them. But there have been many wrong policies from the central government. So we say this: yes, we need technology from outside; investors from outside, but it should be for our mutual interests, not one sided. That is what we say. We have read the United Nations Human Development Report which says that in this process of liberalisation, of globalisation, of privatisation, the poor are not looked after. So we tell our industrialists that we must act together for the development of West Bengal. That we must keep in touch with the workers. And we tell the workers (which we didn't tell them earlier, and I was a trade unionist myself) that you must not only concern yourselves with yourselves but with production and productivity. For if the industry goes down, you go down also. So that is new. I think it is having some effect. This is why foreigners are coming, and the bigger industries of India also. They appreciate the new approach.

PA: Have you been as successful in the great city of Calcutta as you were in the countryside?

JB: The demography of Calcutta has changed. About 50 per cent are outsiders who have come to work here. There are many citizens from other parts of India, and the party has little organisation among them. Therefore we've been losing seats at elections. On the other hand, we've done well municipally, with the Calcutta Corporation. We have a slight majority there.

PA: How well have you been able to control corruption within the party structure?

JB: Somewhat. Within the party. It is there. If you're in power, trying to do the loaves and fishes, there are some opportunists who get in. But we have a system, an organisation which looks after this. We expel members if they are corrupt. Or we prosecute them in the courts. But we have to be ever vigilant because opportunities are always there.

I take him back to his youth in England, in the 1930s, when he was first introduced to the idea of communism.

JB: I didn't belong to a political family. My father was a doctor who came back from America and practised here in Calcutta. We were an upper middle-class family, not interested in politics. I attended missionary schools. But we went to England at the end of 1935 and I stayed there until the end of 1939, returning home in 1940, after the war had started. And those years, of course, were full of stirring events, of remarkable events that were taking place all over the world.

PA: The rise of fascism?

JB: Yes, the rise of fascism, the Spanish Civil War, all of that. And I came upon the Communist Party of Great Britain. It was a small group. It didn't have much influence. But they alone were talking about our independence and our freedom, about the struggle going on in India. So I started reading Marxism and I got interested and I thought that communism was the only way out.

PA: The Freedom Movement had two wings: the Gandhi pacifist movement and yours, the freedom fighters, using violence. Do you agree that Gandhi's contribution, the pacifist contribution to independence, has been overstated?

JB: We say that our history has not been properly written. It is not objective. When you read our history, the official writings, you are told that we were victorious because of non-violent struggles. That is not true. If you read the proceedings in the House of Commons at that time, when Attlee was Prime Minister, you hear them admitting that although they'd won the war, they couldn't keep India. We were determined to liberate ourselves. It's sad that India was divided, that we didn't get the India we'd fought for. We got a split India. But we got our freedom.

We talked of his first elections, as a trade union candidate, a communist candidate.

JB: I got elected from the railway constituency and we got another elected from Darjeeling, a tea trade union constituency.

This was at the time when Australians were voting at a referendum on the Communist Party: should it be banned? Australians, to their own surprise, voted No. But while the Communist Party remained legal in Australia it was banned in India after 1948.

JB: Yes, and we were all taken to prison. We were declared illegal, soon after Independence. We were freedom fighters, just a small force within the Congress. Understand that we'd accepted Congress leadership as the main centre for the freedom fight. But Congress was afraid of us. They thought our influence would spread.

PA: That communism would be a contagion?

JB: Yes. Let us nip it in the bud. But we got our freedom back from the High Court. They declared us a legal party.

PA: You've spent a lot of time in jail over the years. I think you've been in jail six times.

JB: Yes, I was always being detained without trial. Now I need some rest.

PA: You were never convicted of any crime?

JB: No. We had an act, we have it now, where you can detain people without trial. It is very undemocratic. We have never used it in West Bengal.

PA: Have you ever retrieved your files from the security organisations and read them? To see what they were saying about you?

JB: I have seen them the last time I was in Delhi. I was curious to know what they had written about me. It was rubbish.

PA: The Communist Party is, of course, a secular organisation. But to be successful you must gather support from the various religious groupings. Are there many Hindus and Muslims within the CP?

JB: Oh yes, very many. All kinds of people, with their own religions, are with us. The working class is divided in that sense. They belong to this religion or that religion, yet they come to the Communist Party or the trade unions. As you know, our constitution provides for secularism. But politics should not be mixed up with religion. We adhere to that. Of course we have our own philosophies, our own ideas, but we welcome Hindus, Muslims, protected castes, the tribes, and so on.

PA: Across the Western world, and in the ruins of what was the Soviet Union, we see the rise of the extreme right. In the West we fear that this is now happening in India. Yet the current line in your media is that the BJP will have to moderate their line, that they'll have to be careful, middle-of-the-road. Are you relaxed about the BJP?

JB: Not at all. We are very perturbed about what is happening. They got a majority of thirteen and formed a government. We call it a communal party, a fundamentalist party. Its program is quite different. They intend to build a temple in a place where they destroyed a mosque. At the end of the twentieth century this is not civilised. But understand that 63 per cent *did not* vote for the BJP. But they were split among different parties, groups and individuals. That has to be corrected. It is wrong that the BJP, with just 25 per cent of the votes, has gained power.

PA: They call you the boss of Bengal. Yet in your eighties you were going to leave this job, this city, and go to Delhi to run the country.

JB: Yes, I was offered, two years ago, the job of Prime Minister. Thirteen parties had got together and they had nobody. And they thought that I could do it. Not that I was a genius, but that I had experience for so many years. That I understand about coalition.

PA: But your party vetoed the decision, and it's quite obvious that you were disappointed.

JB: I think they made a mistake. But I didn't go to Delhi.

PA: So even at this stage in your extraordinary career, even at your great age, you still accept party discipline?

JB: Yes, as long as I'm in the party.

PA: And how long will you be in the party?

JB: Well, I cannot say, like the brook that 'men will come and men will go, but I go on forever'. There is a time when one has to retire.

PA: And you're contemplating that now?

JB: I am.

PA: Is there a clear successor?

JB: I am waiting for the party congress.

PA: You'll make an announcement then?

JB: I will talk to my colleagues.

PA: You seem to be greatly admired. I found few in Calcutta who speak ill of you.

JB: I am very thankful but there are people who are against me.

PA: You were very close to Indira Gandhi and Rajiv was fond of you. He called you 'Uncle'.

JB: Yes, not in the beginning, but later. He wasn't a politician, you know. He was a pilot. Not interested in politics. But Indira Gandhi couldn't trust anybody else. So she brought her son in. But he didn't know anything. But he was learning quick, that I must say. But it was very unfortunate that he was killed.

PA: Can Sonia Gandhi learn quick?

JB: Yes, but she was a housewife. The Congress is in such a plight that they've requested her to come to the leadership. I said why not? She's an Indian citizen and housewife. We offer 33 per cent reservations for women in the elections to Parliament and the state assemblies.

PA: Over the years I've spoken to many men and women of your age who've been powerful in society. And towards the end of their lives they've become very lonely because, one by one, their friends have died. They are left alone with their memories.

JB: One is born, one grows, one dies. The next generations take over. That is the nature of the human race.

PA: Do you still have contemporaries who were with you in the 1930s, 1940s and 1950s?

JB: Some. But fewer and fewer.

PA: Are you concerned about death?

JB: I don't think about it. One has to die some time. Man is mortal.

PA: Finally, how would you describe yourself. As an intellectual within the Communist Party? As a survivor? What has been your role?

JB: There have been bigger intellectuals in my party than myself. But one has to be a sort of intellectual. As I said, Marxism is a science and you have to study it. And you have to study economics, philosophy and so on. You have to apply them in the concrete situation in your country.

PA: So you still believe that Marxism is a science?

JB: Yes, I do.

PA: Not an art? A science?

JB: It is a science. But mistakes have been committed and we have to learn from those mistakes. I don't know when, but our conception of society will come. Socialism! Communism! It is the splendid objective that we have. Jesus said, 'Love thy neighbour as thyself.' But it didn't happen. We've been fighting each other. When it will come, how it will come, I cannot say. But we hope for it.

10

Astrologers

I read in one of a host of daily newspapers that India's famous astrologer, Balwant Maharaja Ji Parambhakthanumanji, will be at the Hotel Swiss Palace in Room 202.

'Babaji has arrived from Kashi,' says the ad. 'Bajabi whose Bhakti's incredible manifestation tells by looking at your face/ photograph. Through medium of Bhakti, he guides you towards attaining success in business, acquiring wealth, employment, promotion to overcome obstacles in politics, going abroad, studies and problems due to domestic instability, illness etc. Only those with pure intention need to consult the Babaji. He had predicted a lot of film stars their future. You can also avail such golden opportunity.'

Sadly he's entirely booked out. There is no hope of accommodating a visiting sceptic. So we drive across town to visit a seer of comparable reputation, one whose clientele comes, these days, from the masses. I push between some sacred cows, cross a tiny courtyard full of broken pot plants and squeeze into his modest waiting room. It's like going to the doctor, except that there are no old magazines to read. People sit very, very still, looking at the ceiling or floor. Smells of cooking intrude from the astrologer's kitchen, and a little child waddles in, only to be scooped up by a sari'd mother.

While I wait I leaf through the paper that reported the whereabouts of Babaji.

'WITCH' KILLED BY SON AND NEPHEW IN MALDA

A 45-year-old tribal woman, suspected of being a witch, was killed by her son and nephew at Gajol in the Malda district on Thursday, reports PTI.

The victim, Sumi Mardi, had told a villager, suffering from fever, to see a registered doctor instead of going to quacks. This apparently gave rise to the suspicion that she was a witch, delayed reports said here today.

The victim's son and nephew, Sailen and Sukul Mardi, murdered her with a pickaxe. They cut the body to pieces before surrendering to Gajol police station.

'She turned out to be witched and we finished her,' the two told police.

The newspapers abound in stories of violent death, but this was one of the oddest. A woman is killed as a witch because she urges a villager to avoid quackery, which in India is invariably mystical quackery. In other words, she was killed as a witch because she warned against witchcraft.

The hold on the Indian mind by medieval quackeries is almost as startling as the influence of New Age nonsense on Californians. But it is nothing to the influence on senior politicians by the sayers of sooths. In America, the wealthy have therapists. In India, they've astrologers. Like Ronald Reagan, India Gandhi sought the guidance of the stars and India's nuclear physicists consult them before conducting bomb tests.

The assassination of Rajiv Gandhi produced as many conspiracy theories as JFK's. As you know, the only person in America who had nothing, absolutely nothing to do with the killing of Kennedy was Oswald. He either wasn't there or, if he was, he was just 'the patsy'. It is now painfully clear that the President was murdered by the CIA, the Mafia, the FBI, Lyndon Johnson, aliens and Jacqueline after an insurance pay-out. But not necessarily in that order.

Conspiracy theories are just as prevalent in India. Take the assassination of Rajiv Gandhi in the Tamil Nadu town of Sriperumbudur in 1991. Officialdom would have us believe that he was targeted by Sri Lankan separatists. But everyone knows it was organised by a cabal of his predecessors aided and abetted by a Hindu guru with the mellifluous name of Chandraswami. A plump, white-bearded little bloke incandescent with psychic powers, he's billed as the Indian counterpart to Rasputin. And he's been saying sooths for major players in Indian politics for thirty years.

His co-conspirators in the killing of Rajiv Gandhi are, according to those in the know, not one, not two, but three former prime ministers — Chandra Shekhar, Vishwanath Pratap Singh and P.V. Narasimha Rao. The woman who blew Gandhi and herself to pieces was as innocent as Oswald. Another patsy.

Needless to say these facts are disputed by duplicitous officialdom. After investigating the allegations for years, Judge Milap Chand Jain has come up with one of those official whitewashes. 'By no stretch of the imagination can it be said that any of them [that is, the former premiers] entertained any such intention to be in any way connected with the conspiracy to assassinate Rajiv Gandhi.'

His pronouncement convinces nobody.

In considering the central role of Chandraswami, the Rasputin of Delhi, let us remember that Indian politicians are not alone in their passion for paranormal pollsters. We know that Ronald Reagan wouldn't go to the bathroom without Nancy taking advice from a favourite necromancer. Not for Reagan the psychoanalyst. Nancy would book him into his psychic analyst. You'll recall that Reagan was sworn in as Governor of California at midnight, because their San Franciscan seer regarded this as the most propitious of times. And his negotations with Gorbachev were subjected to mystic monitoring.

While we can reject rumours that John Howard is overly influenced by Athena Starwoman, or that Margaret Thatcher invited Doris Stokes to Downing Street, we cannot patronise the Indian political hierarchy for transcendental enthusiasms. And Chandraswami is, by all accounts, a compelling presence who's been called in by such spiritual seekers as Saudi arms dealer Adnan Khashoggi, Hollywood legend Elizabeth Taylor and the Sultan of Brunei. He also served Mr Rao who succeeded Gandhi as PM.

Having received the long-awaited report from Judge Milap Chand Jain, the government has formed a panel to look into the role of the Chandraswami who will, of course, already have predicted its outcome.

Finally, it's my turn to sit across the desk from a chain-smoking practitioner of paranormal skills. His inner sanctum is dominated by a large desk leaving very little room for him, let alone me. Add a couple of mike stands and we were pressed against the walls which, once again, are covered with a collection of framed images that are not simply eclectic but eccentric. Behold the usual collision of cultures — images of saints from any number of faiths — cheek-by-jowl with secular portraits, landscapes and Hindu calendars.

He stubs a butt in an overflowing ashtray and takes my hand in his, running a finger saffron'd with nicotine over the creases in my palm. His eyes squint from the smoke. Between hacking coughs he gazes at my palm. Is 'mumbo jumbo' an Indian term? Sounds like it. If so, it is entirely lacking here. No mumbo, no jumbo, just a brisk assessment of my personality and prospects. I hoped to get a full confession from the guru, as well as a glimpse into my own future.

He begins by having me spell out my surname.

Astrologer: A, d?

PA: A, m.

Astrologer: M?

PA: Yes, M. M for mystic. And S for spiritual.

Astrologer: Yes.

PA: I would like you to tell me what you can about me.

Astrologer: About you? In accordance with astrological point of view, our palmist point of view, you're a happy chap. You're a self-made man. Your palm says this. In this way. You possess a good headline. Yes, a good headline. The man who possesses such a type of good headline ...

PA: A good headline? This is about the mind? The brain?

Astrologer: Indicates good luck also. The man who possesses this type of mound [he presses my palm with his finger] indicates that his life is successful in spite of having several difficulties that come from several origins and several ways. With several troubles. You'll be the successful candidate undoubtedly. In spite of your several difficulties. This is a good line. You are an established gentleman. Much will be accomplished by the holy grace of God. And you are a religious-minded man also.

PA: I'm a religious-minded man?

Astrologer: Yes. Much will be accomplished by the holy grace of God. Your good mound says so. As does this line.

PA: What line?

Astrologer: This line. It is called Fortune Line.

PA: Oh, the Fortune Line. Right.

Astrologer: The man who possesses this type of fortune line also indicates that his life will be successful. Are you a businessman at present?

PA: No, I'm not a businessman. At present.

Astrologer: But an established gentleman? Take a good and great job?

PA: Yes, I've taken a good and great job. To expiate guilts for past lives.

Astrologer: Yes, this is true. You have taken a good position. Are you in Australia at present?

PA: No, I'm in India. But I'm usually in Australia.

Astrologer: Having taken a great and good job you are an established gentleman. You have several cars and a house.

PA: Yes, I have several cars and a house. I've also got a very dirty hand. I'm sorry. I should have washed it before I came here.

Astrologer: Matters not. Your hand indicates the forecast which I am giving at present. Is what I say perfect or not?

PA: Absolutely perfect. Can you tell me anything about children?

Astrologer: Yes. At present you have several.

PA: Quite true, quite true. And the future?

Astrologer: After 16 September your disturbances will go away? Can you follow?

PA: Not exactly.

Astrologer: At present, several difficulties may come. But the difficulties may go away after 16 September.

PA: Well that's an enormous relief. What about longevity? Can you tell me whether I'll still be alive this time next year?

Astrologer: I will break tea.

PA: Okay, we're breaking for tea.

Astrologer: You have very good mounds. This one here. And this one. That's why you can expect the longevity of life. You can expect the longevity of life up to eighty-four to eighty-six years.

PA: That's good. Incidentally, how many years are you?

Astrologer: At present I'm sixty-seven.

PA: You look younger. Do you have a urine regimen?

Astrologer: No, I pray to God and I take my meditation several times also.

PA: Thanks for the tea. Delicious. I notice that you have a picture of Jesus Christ above you.

Astrologer: I love him from the core of my heart because at the time of my difficulties I have gone several places to work on my difficulties. But there is no man who will come to help me. But at one moment one night I have seen him.

PA: You've seen Jesus?

Astrologer: 'Don't be worry about your problems,' Jesus said.

PA: Jesus said this to you?

Astrologer: I must tell.

PA: You're very fortunate.

Astrologer: I saw him visually.

PA: This is a rare experience.

Astrologer: More tea?

PA: Thank you. You have a very busy practice.

Astrologer: Because people believe me from the core of their heart. I have several Christian friends also. They come. Several questions.

PA: Were you born with this gift?

Astrologer: My father was Bengali people and Hindu by caste. I am not Hindu by caste. But Jesus Christ is like my god. He is here and he must tell me.

PA: Jesus has helped you become a soothsayer?

Astrologer: I have seen him several times and don't mind at all when I am with him.

PA: This is curious. It would be a remarkable event anywhere in the Christian world. But for someone of a Hindu background to be instructed by Jesus is ... you are most fortunate.

Astrologer: I don't understand it. On several occasions friends have said, 'A Hindu like you who likes the goddess Kali?' I tell myself that Jesus loves me well.

PA: You do astrological charts. Is Indian astrology the same as Western astrology?

Astrologer: No, there are several difficulties. Indian astrology takes one side. European astrology takes another. Some big differences may come. Show me your thumb.

PA: My thumb?

Astrologer: This is also a good sign. On your thumb.

PA: There is something on my thumb?

Astrologer: Yes. Are you a director in a company?

PA: Yes.

Astrologer: In Australia?

PA: Yes.

Astrologer: I thought so.

PA: So I've got a sign on my thumb which says I'm a company director?

Astrologer: God will help you. At time of several difficulties you will think about God and he will help you.

PA: Will I be successful in marriage?

Astrologer: Yes. No.

PA: Yes and no?

Astrologer: Yes. At present you will be a successful candidate. So says this mound. Then you will not be so successful.

PA: And further children?

Astrologer: Your mind will not permit the same.

PA: My mind?

Astrologer: No, your mound.

PA: Thank you for your time. Before I go, a question.

	Do you have clients in government? Do you talk to politicians?
Astrologer:	I have had several times also. But I don't go there. I don't go there. Because waste of time.
PA:	A waste of time to talk to politicians?
Astrologer:	If I go to the present Prime Minister. If he calls me to go there. A waste of time.

Here endeth the lesson. We then decamp to the kitchen for more *chay* with his wife, his daughter, his unemployed son-in-law and a newly born grandchild who looked at me with the sort of wisdom you'd expect from the latest member of a mystical dynasty.

The seer had been immensely bored by the proceedings. It must be a heavy burden to know everything, and to know it in advance. With the future mapped out like a street directory you'd never be surprised by anything. You'd live in a constant state of deja vu. There hadn't been a hint of the theatrical. Once my hand was in his he couldn't have been more off-hand. It was take it or leave it. And given his considerable reputation, it was obvious that most people took it.

All in all, a moving experience. A bit like getting a quote from a plumber. And I leave reassured that I'll live to eighty-four or eighty-six, that my mind or my mound will act as a contraceptive, that things will be fine after September and that I have a thumb which is a business indicator. Not bad for a couple of dollars.

The encounter made me more determined to track down the Indian Skeptics, one of the country's bravest groups. Like the Australian Skeptics, of which I was a co-founder, the group is connected to CSICOP in New York — the Committee for the Scientific Investigation of Claims of Paranormal. They send hit squads into remote villages where psychic frauds use tawdry conjuring tricks to awe the gullible ... and consequently to exercise an enormous amount of control over their lives. The sceptics will replicate the tricks — producing the same explosions of coloured powder, palming the same costume jewellery — and the villagers will be astonished. Then they might start to question the credentials of the psychic quacks who dominated their lives for millennia. To surrender to fatalism is to yield to tyranny and exploitation. But the sceptics are out of town, presumably confronting another psychic fraud.

The mystical mumbo jumbo that so enchants the tourist is, like the caste system, a source of repression. Tell people that everything in their lives in predestined, fated, and you encourage acquiescence to the status quo. You undermine the ability of people to question, to organise, to work for changes in their lives. And the sheisters and shonks who work the villages, and the political masters in Delhi, are an unlovely group. Like Chandraswami their influence is as excessive as it's grotesque. They can become puppet masters to the most powerful people in the land.

To be a sceptic in India is to fight a losing battle. It's like driving a little red fire cart around Hades.

11

Cemeteries

Now dead, Brian Robinson was my oldest, dearest friend. A film-maker, and artist, founder of the Swinburne Film School, he was a man of fastidious intelligence and proved over the years to be the best of travelling companions with a great gift for observation and subsequent embellishment. Not content with mere anecdotes, he created formidable fictions from the business of living. And his eye for art was as good as his gift for narrative.

On a trip to India we'd found a row of antique shops in a back street that were jumbled with wonderful things: Christian carvings from Goa, saints and Virgins that hybridised the Indian with the European, battered Ganeshas in wood, bronze and ivory, an entire temple doorway, ruined portraits of minor princelings. Every dusty nook and cobwebbed cranny was a niche for another god from the vast Hindu menagerie, many of them charged with the sanctity that only age bestows. Moreover, they were ludicrously cheap.

We were looking at a group of sitars, inlaid with ivory, with the bulbous resonators like nut-brown versions of the spaceship in Kubrick's *2001*. Little use as instruments, they were marvellous as sculptures, and only ten, twenty dollars each.

While plucking a wonky string, Brian announced his intention of chucking it all in. He'd leave Swinburne, sell his house and spend the rest of his life travelling. 'A month in Venice, a couple of months in Peru.'

In that instant, I had an image of all the cemeteries we'd visited over the years, of the expatriate graves we'd found, and how intensely lonely they had seemed. Even in the most beautiful cemeteries, like Venice's, the foreign dead looked doubly forgotten, doubly dead. As forlorn as flotsam in the canals.

'But don't you have a dread of dying in a foreign hospital?' I asked. I was about to add, 'And finishing up in a foreign cemetery', when he interrupted. 'Phillip, every hospital is a foreign country. Even the hospitals in Hawthorn.'

He was, of course, absolutely right.

He's been dead now for five or six years. Had a heart attack in David Jones and died in the Royal Melbourne. And I'm sad to say I can't remember where he was buried, or if he was buried. Perhaps his brothers took his ashes back to Mildura or his Melbourne friends scattered them in his beloved Botanic Gardens, by the Yarra.

Although an atheist, Brian would have liked to have been burnt on the *ghats* at Varanasi. Failing that he'd have enjoyed knowing that he had a plot in a cemetery I've just discovered in Calcutta. Either outcome would have amused him. He had no fear of the foreign.

I've been collecting cemeteries for forty years. As I've travelled around Australia and the world I've found some great ones, such as the boneyard near Montmartre where Oscar Wilde finished up after a losing battle with some notorious wallpaper. Like the old Jewish cemetery in Prague, a ghetto for the dead, so crowded that the headstones seem to be squeezed from their plots. Like Highgate in London, and, of course, the island cemetery at Venice which Diaghilev shares with Nijinsky and Ezra Pound.

And this one in Calcutta? Absolutely of the first rank. You'd be delighted to be dead here. But unfortunately burials are no longer available. You had to be a member of the Raj to be planted in the South Park Street Cemetery, known throughout India as 'the Great Cemetery', the most important of its kind in the East.

It's hidden behind a high wall surrounded by high-rise buildings and looming, decrepit advertising hordings. And if you can gain entry (the gate is padlocked but opened from time to time) you find yourself among immense monuments to the departed of the Raj who were brought here for their eternal rest.

There are graves going back to the early 1700s, and the sepulchral monuments are like nothing else you'll ever see. For quite apart from their immense scale there isn't a hint that Christians are buried here. Not a hint. After an hour or more I found only one cross, and a small one. It was as if all the crucifixes had been smashed off, or carted away over the centuries by disapproving members of other faiths.

I remember a similar feeling of curiosity and surprise in the cemetery in Melbourne where a number of my family has been filed, awaiting Judgment Day. The Kew Cemetery bristles with Christian iconography, yet in the middle of it there's a monument to paganism marking the last resting place of, of all people, David Syme, founding father of the Melbourne *Age*. His tomb is of the Egyptian style, encrusted with bronze scarabs and cobras, an eternal affront to the Christian crosses and angels of Kew's Bundoora Cemetery. Did Mr Syme have a Pharaonic ego? Or did he belong to a cult? None of the Syme family could proffer an explanation.

(The fathers of Australian Federation were as enthralled by the paranormal as the Reagans. Prime Minister Barton and many of his bearded mates, including Syme, embraced everything from theosophy to the ouija board.)

And what is the explanation for the absence of Christian iconography here in Calcutta?

The cemetery is full of dead soldiers, either killed in skirmishes with the natives or laid low by disease. They are blood brothers to the Christian soldiers whose tombs fill Westminster Abbey, members of God's top brass. Why, then, is the South Park a crucifix-free zone? Where have all the angels flown?

No, it wasn't vandalism or cultural sensitivities that eliminated the angel or the crucifix. It was, it seems, simply a case of funereal fashion. The architecture of the mausoleum developed at the time of Beethoven and Nash when a love of classicism in Britain was exported with imperial ambitions. Thus graceful Roman cupolas, elegant Grecian urns and abbreviated obelisks proliferated, along with some Roman and Etruscan-style sarcophagi above the ground. Here lies Colonel Charles Russell Deare, who fought in North America and the West Indies, and was slain by a cannon ball while fighting Tippoo Sultan in the

Carnatic, while a finely proportioned stone column marks the last resting place of the twenty-six-year-old Captain Cooke, who was also commemorated in Westminster Abbey. He died from wounds suffered during an epic sea fight in the mouth of the Hoogly in which he captured the French frigate, *La Forte*, released the English sailors held prisoner on board, and brought back the battered hulk as a prize to Calcutta.

All is solid, serene and confident, in contrast to the dangerous times of the monuments' construction. Yet for all their classicism the tombs are inescapably Indian, in the way their domes seem to distend into stupas.

All hail the Association for the Preservation of Historical Cemeteries in India, a branch of the British Association for Cemeteries in South Asia. It is they who have saved these graves from an early grave, who have raised the money that has, at very least, delayed the cemetery's death. It seems that only a few years ago the place was a medley of unkempt tombs and undergrowth. The walls were tumbling down and the tombs were being either vandalised or used 'by thieves to store their loot', while vagrants, braving the snakes and rabid dogs, shared the tombs with their approved inhabitants.

These days most of us end up in a copper urn, or in a lawn cemetery devoid of statuary of likable melancholia. There you're lucky to get a brass plaque big enough for your name, rank and serial number. But here you get an inkling of the life story of the deadun, albeit in hagiographic terms.

UNDERNEATH HERE LIE THE REMAINS OF CAPTAIN ANTHONY HUNT, CAPTAIN IN THE ROYAL NAVY WHO DEPARTED THIS LIFE ON 10th DAY OF AUGUFT 1798 AFTER A SHORT ILLNESS IN THE 28TH YEAR OF HIS AGE.

He did well, didn't he? To be a captain so young.

AND WHO AT THIS EARLY AGE HAD ACQUIRED GREAT HONOURS IN HIS PROFESSION, AND THE ESTEEM AND REGARD OF ALL WHO HAD THE HONOUR OF HIS ACQUAINTANCE. BY HIS DEATH, THE NAVY HAS LOST ONE OF ITS BRIGHTEST ORNAMENTS, AND SOCIETY ONE OF ITS MOST VALUABLE MEMBERS, FOR HE LIVED

> GREATLY BELOVED AND RESPECTED, AND DIED UNIVERSALLY REGRETTED.

Now, that's what I call a decent epitaph.

The thing that wealth gives people, apart from privilege, and choice, is space. And space is the most precious thing in a place like Calcutta. It's unavailable for the living, who lie in cheek-by-jowl proximity with each other without even the notion of privacy. But even in death, the Raj had room to move. Within walls worthy of a prison, the South Park Street Cemetery must cover more than a hectare. The avenues are wide and now that the place has been cleared of thieves, vagrants and most of the snakes and dogs, the members of the Raj enjoy posthumous privilege.

I'm sure they wouldn't mind all the cricket matches being played here. There's a small hole in a distant wall that the local kids have turned to their advantage. No less than ten cricket matches are being played here simultaneously, using the avenues as pitches and headstones for wickets. From time to time I've had to duck as a cricket ball has ricocheted from an obelisk. I'm sure the deceased gentle folk were all devotees of cricket, the men entering the oval through the 'Gentlemen' gate as opposed to the 'Players', while the women sat beneath their parasols sipping tea from Royal Doulton.

Isn't this what cemeteries should be about? About the intermingling of life and death? If so, on this occasion, thanks to the cricket playing, life is batting and likely to win by quite a few runs.

This cemetery is a branch of the East India Company, otherwise known as 'the honourable company', and referred to as such on many a tomb.

> HERE REPOSE THE EARTHLY REMAINS OF MR JAMES MILLER, LAST MINT MASTER OF THE HONOURABLE COMPANY, WHO DEPARTED THIS LIFE 7 JULY 1799 IN THE 54TH YEAR OF HIS AGE.

It didn't seem to matter what your rank was in the company, or in the army that protected it. Whether you wrapped parcels or commanded cavalry you got a stupefying monument. There are few small monuments here.

Childbirth was the major cause of death for the young women here. Infant mortality was appalling for all classes. As it remains for the poor of India almost two centuries later. Here, for example, is a tomb containing the remains of four infant children of the Twisden family who died between 1820 and 1827. The oldest of them survived for just one year and ten months. I wonder what the infant mortality rate is in the slums of Calcutta? Typical of the women who died here was Mrs Martha Goodlad whose epitaph reads 'departed this life on 21st March 1785 aged 23'.

Tis said that the British are emotionally inhibited. Not so. The outpouring of grief we witnessed over the death of Princess Diana was presaged here, two centuries earlier in stone.

If ever tears deservedly were shed;
If ever grief was due to virtue dead;
Thy merit, Martha, and thy spotleff ways
Claim tears from all, for allowed them praise.
Thy strength of mind we scarce shall meet again,
Shoon through a long, most agonising pain,
Thy warm affections of wife or friend,
Make all who knew you weep your cruel end.
Cruel alas, but this one thing was sure:
Those virtues that in life you held so pure
Will be repaid. This thought, and this alone
Your friends are left to mitigate them, moan.
This latest tribute a kind husband gives
Whose heart is torn and wretched while he lives
And only prays one day to reach that shore
To meet his Martha and to part no more.

There are other chiselled obituaries that seem to have been written by Jane Austen. In between writing screenplays for Hollywood.

To walk through this cemetery is to walk around a huge chess board, among giant chess pieces. There are kings, there are queens, there are bishops and there are any number of knights. But no pawns. And there are more mysteries than the missing crucifixes. Take the largest tomb of all, one of truly imperial, Ramesean dimensions, a tomb that rises up and up and up, reaching to the polluted skies of Calcutta. Why is it entirely anonymous?

'Here was deposited,' it says, 'the mortal part of a man who feared God but not death, and maintained independence but sought not riches, who thought none below him, but that he found unjust, none above, but the wise and virtuous, who loved his parents, kindred, friends, country, with an ardour' (I love that word) 'which was the chief source of all his pleasures and all his pains, and who having devoted his life to their service and to the improvement of his memory and his mother's pride. Beloved he lived, and lamented died.'

Behold the Unknown Soldier.

'Ardour' is just one of the many anachronistic words in the vocabulary of this necropolis. Others include 'fidelity', 'integrity' and 'distinguished'. Clearly there was a different language for public life. These days very few could expect such accolades. Perhaps Sir William Deane when he kicks the bucket.

In Australia, we bulldoze cemeteries for car parks. I remember that happening when I lived at Oakleigh in Melbourne. In the spirit of the level playing field they levelled the boneyard and poured asphalt all over it. Mind you, that's a proud Victorian tradition — the original Melbourne Cemetery lies deep beneath the stalls of the Victoria Market. When I heard that they were crushing the headstones I rushed to the scene of desecration in the hope of salvaging one of them, my favourite. A severe, simple piece of stone with the most enigmatic of inscriptions: 'This is Ellen's grave'. That was all it had said. No surname, no date. No words of consolation or regret. I was going to take Ellen home and plonk her in the garden but by the time I got there the municipality had murdered her memory.

But in India, in Calcutta, arguably the most crowded city on Earth, despite all the population pressures, despite the immense pushing and shoving for every inch of space, this cemetery is preserved, protected, nurtured.

And here's another mystery. The cemetery seems unpolluted. In total contrast to the suffocations of the city a pleasant zephyr blows through here. Instead of filtering the smog with your hankie, you dare to take a deep breath.

Almost everything that survives from the ancient world is death related, either tombs or things that were placed in tombs, from mummies to pottery. The ordinary dwellings, like those of the lower ranks who saw the pyramids being raised, or helped raise them, are long gone, although you can find traces of the mudbrick buildings on the plains of Giza. The powerful dead, like the powerful living, could always depend on the poor for cheap labour. In India this means that even a low-ranking officer, an underling in the honourable company, could afford to dwell forever, or for as much as forever as the monsoons allowed, in a stonemason'd mansion after death. There must have been more humble tombs here. But they've gone, leaving just the domes, the mastaba and the obelisks.

Is inflexibility in principle, or indeed in anything, such a good thing? It was certainly important to the people who planted Colonel George Hickson here. It seems that George was 'inflexible in principle and poffessed in an eminent degree, the qualities which command respect and ensure success in public life'. All his family are beside him, the whole lot of them, in a huge tomb overwhelmed by the arse end, the backside of tilting advertising hoardings. On one side there are signs advertising Pepsi, or the latest Swami who's arrived in town.

On one side of the cemetery there's a wailing wall of salvaged headstones that belonged to graves that have long since disintegrated. Here I discover the one occupant of South Park with an Indian-sounding name: Vanistart. Perhaps an Anglo-Indian, Vanistart was employed by the Bengal Civil Service. He died in 1807, at just thirty-three years of age, presumably exhausted by the paperwork. Everyone else is a pom who, like Vanistart, died young. So young that thirty-three years amounts to a ripe old age.

Aurelius Khan, one of the selfless committee members who have fought to save this place from decay and/or development, wrote the following plea in 1978:

Art, it has been said, is history made organic. While some may cavil at the claim of sepulchral monuments to be called art, none may doubt that graves and funerary relics, by giving substance to the sentiments, customs and beliefs of a people, shed light on the measure of their civilisation. Archaeology owes no small debt to the remains of the dead found in the burial grounds of antiquity.

Less hallowed by age but of no mean historical interest are the tombs and mausolea looming in the old cemeteries of Calcutta in memory of the Europeans who spent their short span in a distant land, many for gain, some for glory or in service of their country, a few for their faith, others to keep the King's peace or enrich an ancient culture with offerings of their own. These sentinels of the past speak silently of the way of life, the habits, hopes and fears of a generation that walked and talked in the once fevered expanse of this city a century or two ago. For posterity to permit total eclipse of the testimony of their existence would be to lose surely the sense of history without which the story of mankind would be poor indeed.

When the people who are buried here arrived in Calcutta it was a small city busying itself with trade. In the beginning there were few lofty ceilings or aerial verandahs, and the immigrants had no immunity to tropical disease and fevers. For others there was the mental stagnation of a small society, which intensified both nostalgia and loneliness. Perhaps this was hardest to bear.

Burials invariably took place after dark with the light of torches, the coffin generally carried on the shoulders of the deceased's friends. Frequently there was the pageantry of a military funeral, and the sound of the minute guns following across from Fort William. Around the cemetery, in the beginning, stood a bamboo forest and Warren Hastings, towards the end of the eighteenth century, hunted tiger there.

Here's one of the tallest monuments, dedicated to the memory of Sir William Jones, the founder of the Royal Asiatic Society of Bengal. He possessed such a linguistic genius that he was reputed to have mastered every European language, in addition to various Oriental languages, except that of his own country. Yes, Sir William Jones was a Welshman.

There are a number of Armenian graves in the cemetery. The Armenians were invited to Calcutta by Job Charnock, the city's founder, and the Hon'ble Company extended its protection to the Armenian church.

Here lies the last remains of Major General Charles Stuart, known as 'Hindu Stuart'. Quite remarkably, the Major General became a Hindu and used to walk from his home every morning to bathe in the Hooghly River. When he went on leave to England he took with him many images of Hindu deities and performed religious rites there. This tomb was once surmounted by an elaborate edifice with stone carvings of deities. Presumably his defection from the Christian ranks was characterised as a harmless eccentricity. Otherwise they wouldn't have let him through the gates.

Henry Louis Vivian Derozio, a famous Anglo-Indian poet and reformer, who died at the age of twenty-two, is buried here. They say his style echoed Byron's. Other eternal residents with literary connections include Lucia Palk, the heroine of Kipling's *Concerning Licia*, and Rose Aylmer, muse for the poet Landor when they wandered the mountains and shores of Wales. She died of cholera within a year of arriving in Calcutta and the heartbroken Landor quilled his famous *Ode to Rose*.

Queen Victoria said in one of her letters that there was scarcely a family of prominence in Britain which had not one or more younger sons serving in India. And it seems that many of those younger sons, or the even younger wives, remained in her service here, lying stiffly to attention in their coffins.

In marked contrast to this splendid cemetery is the piece of open ground on the outskirts of Calcutta where people, poor people, simply dump bodies. Because they can't afford to take a corpse to a *ghat* or even to the municipal incinerator. There's a row about the place at the moment, not because of the bodies that are left there for the dogs and the crows, but because of the city's intention of building a police station smack in the middle of it. In a city of twenty million people, of grinding poverty, thousands must be dying every week. Quite a few are found floating in the Hoogly but it must require immense ingenuity of the bereaved to find a nook, a cranny, a dumpster.

The Calcutta Municipal Corporation intends to commission

an electric crematorium for the unclaimed bodies. It will have two furnaces. The CMC will hire private lorries to collect bodies from the hospitals and police morgues, and it's planned to construct an air-conditioned building adjacent to the crematorium to store them. However this will only be done after more funds are available. At present all unclaimed bodies are buried at the Hindu burial ground at Topsia. A gas oven, which had been used to cremate the bodies at the burial ground during British rule, has been lying non-functional for the past forty years.

So life goes on. Ditto death.

12

How to Achieve Serenity in the Slammer

Six Criminals Lynched at Sandeshkhali

Six criminals were lynched by villagers at Daudpur in the Sandeshkhali area of North 24-Parganas on Saturday night, police said today.

The criminals, who came from Canning in South 24 Parganas, approached Bhola Mondal, a villager, and sought shelter in his house for the night. They told Bhola they had come from Canning and were scheduled to return the same day. But because of a disruption in launch services in the area, they could not reach the return ferry.

They said they were new to the place and could not afford hotel charges. Bhola let them to stay at his house.

According to the North 24-Parganas SP, the men had a dispute with Bhola's father over control of a bheri in the locality. The criminals then beat up Bhola and his father. Police said Bhola was also a criminal.

The villagers, on hearing a commotion, assembled near

Bhola's house. When they saw Bhola and his father being beaten up they raised an alarm and chased the five criminals out of the house.

These five criminals were soon caught by the villagers at Hatkhola and beaten to death. Police reached the spot on Sunday morning and found Bhola's body. The other five bodies were later found in different parts of the village.

Newspapers abound with stories of similar crimes, and the jails are full of people who commit them. Tihar, with its 10,000 prisoners, is one of the biggest prisons in all Asia and was, until recently, one of the most notorious. Ninety per cent of its inmates, at any one time, are awaiting trial. It's not uncommon to wait six years for a minor charge, like pickpocketing and, finally, to receive a one-year sentence.

Close to New Delhi, Tihar is surrounded by eucalypts and contains four separate jails beset with all the usual problems: gang fights, corruption and drugs. All intensified by overcrowding.

Then Kirin Bedi arrived. Bedi, with her close-cropped hair and lacerating smile, looks like Liza Minnelli in *Cabaret*. Born in Amritsar, Punjab, in 1949, she received a Bachelors in English from the Government College for Women, a Masters in Political Science from Punjab University, a Law degree from the University of Delhi and a Doctorate in Social Sciences from Delhi's Indian Institute of Science. She also found time to be an All India and All Asia tennis champion, having won the Asian Ladies' title at the age of twenty-two. And in 1972, Bedi became the first woman admitted to the Indian police service.

The indefatigable Bedi worked in every aspect of modern-day policing, including narcotics, traffic and VIP security. And she arrived at Tihar determined to turn it into an *ashram*.

'There were acute problems of overcrowding, inadequate sanitation, insufficient breathing space,' she recalls. 'The jail staff had been trained under the old rules where the outlook was to oppress, deprive, isolate and punish. The staff believed that oppressing and imposing maximum restrictions on the inmates would make them suffer, so that once a prisoner was released he would not commit crimes again for fear of being sent back to this hell. But they were mistaken. After their release many prisoners did return, and some prisoners incarcerated for petty crimes resorted to more serious crimes, having learned in Tihar to become bigger and better criminals. Tihar was breeding criminals, not reformed citizens.'

The Superintendent of Jail No. 2 talked about Tihar's initiatives. 'Mrs Bedi started a system of direct access by circulating a sealed complaint box once a day, and she made it a point that all complaints were read by her personally on the same day, and action taken immediately. She encouraged the inmates to gather every afternoon and speak their concerns into a public microphone. She told them not to consider her a jail official but, rather, their sister, and the superintendents their brothers. Many took this opportunity to criticise some officers of the administration. No action was taken against them. The result was that, within two months the entire atmosphere at Tihar had changed.'

As well as introducing detoxification programs, improved nutrition and sanitation, Bedi arranged for literacy and language classes to be taught by prisoners. Then she heard of experiments with Vipassana in regional prisons. Based on Buddhist teachings dating back twenty-five centuries, Vipassana was introduced to modern India and the Indian prison system by S.N. Goenka in 1975 when he undertook small-scale experiments in Rajistan, Baroda and Gujarat. The best accounts of what happened come from a documentary *Doing Time, Doing Vipassana* by the Israeli filmmakers Ayelet Menahemi and Eilona Aeriel, yet to find a sympathetic network in Australia.

'Mrs Bedi wanted everyone to feel that prisoners were not rejected by society but were a part of it,' said one of her superintendents, 'and if they were ready to change they would be welcomed with open arms. She told us, "There is little difference between inmates and ourselves, a very small thread. They lost their balance of mind. We have also lost our tempers, but thankfully we are not held inside this prison. I believe everyone, if given a chance, will try and change, and I want to give them that chance."'

Talking to her prisoners in Hindi, Mrs Bedi spoke to me in English, in the crisp, musical English with impeccable diction that you hear from much of the Indian intelligentsia. 'I'd been looking all along for a behavioural methodology that would make a real change,' she said. 'I would say things to the prisoners, and also to my staff, and they went in one ear and out the other. We would spend so much time talking, yet ultimately it made little difference. Then we introduced Vipassana and it went deeply into them. It provided the environment for other reforms to take roots. It made them more at peace with themselves. They became better humans to work with. The Vipassana courses alone brought lasting changes.'

Among the thousand prisoners who attended the initial course in Vipassana were twenty-eight foreign inmates, including prisoners from Germany, Spain, France, Italy, Sri Lanka, Afghanistan, South African, Nigeria, Somalia, Tanzania, Senegal, Canada and Australia. Mrs Bedi told them, 'We will all receive a new direction in our lives. We will find our way, the path. The only thing that remains is to walk on it.'

Uncomfortable with the notion of the guru and hopelessly addicted to stress, I've never sought succour in yoga, let alone self-knowledge in meditation. I know enough of myself to know that I don't want to know more about myself, but my scepticism melted away as I spoke to Kirin Bedi about her remarkable experiment. It has led, she insists, to far lower rates of recidivism, and to the creation of a prison that is well on the way to being transformed.

It is claimed that in ancient times Vispassana turned serial killers into saints. And it all begins with breathing. Apparently you focus on your breath as it comes in and out of the nostrils. I'd be hard pressed to endure ten minutes of this, but the prisoners stuck it out for ten days. For a while memories intrude and the mind wanders. But it seems that after three days your thoughts dim and you go inside into a deep trance. 'After a three-day struggle the mind quiets down. Thoughts become faint, faded like passing clouds. By focusing for so long on the small patch of skin below the nostrils, the mind becomes so sensitive that it can feel the subtlest flow of breath. A new realm of sensations unfolds in this area — itching, tingling, heat, pressure. Natural physical sensations, never before experienced so vividly. Only then is one prepared to learn Vipassana. The whole idea with

Vipassana is to go inside. And when you go inside and everything is quiet, in yourself you're quiet, then you contact yourself, you can come inside yourself, and you can feel your sensations.'

We're told that through Vipassana one realises that one's own attitudes and addictions, suffering and happiness are not caused by the outside world. It is a way of learning responsibility and self-control.

What began in 1993 with one hundred prisoners and prison officers became a course encompassing thousands. The documentary shows a thousand inmates meditating together, in a space made beautiful within the prison with rugs and drapes. A vast space suitable for a wedding. On the first day there was an unseasonable rainstorm which wrecked the tent and drenched the rugs: a catastrophe. But the prisoners worked to repair the damage and by the end of the day were ready to try again.

Imagine a thousand pairs of sandals piled against the wall while, inside, a thousand men, almost all of whom have elaborate, stylish moustaches, sit in white robes on Indian rugs.

Even while talking to Kirin Bedi I can feel my scepticism. This is too good to be true. Yet the film presents the testimony of prisoner after prisoner, including an Australian doing time for drugs. One of them explains, 'In prison there are prison rules. Vipassana has rules. Vipassana's rules are stricter than prison rules.' And he, like hundreds of other prisoners, welcomed the discipline and found the technique transforming.

'Ten days to light a candle. Sometimes the candle doesn't ignite. It doesn't work for everybody. On the morning of the tenth day silence ends and the prisoners embrace each other and the guards. On the first day I felt trapped. On the second day I wanted to run away.'

In the West, the building of prisons seems to be outstripping that of five-star hotels. And the occupancy rates are far more impressive. Victoria is privatising its prisons faster than anywhere else on Earth, so there must be a quid in it. In the US, far and away the world's most enthusiastic jailer of its citizenry, with close to two million people under lock and key, many state governments are spending more on prison cells than classrooms. And you'll hear none of that do-gooder nonsense about rehabilitation. In America, they're putting the pen back into penology, the death back into Death Row. Poor Jeremy Bentham would be turning in his grave, if only he had one. Bentham, who was first stuffed, and then stuffed into a cupboard at London University, can claim to be the inventor of the modern prison, but his noble ideals have been scrapped in favour of raw fear and pure vengeance.

Australian politicians energetically participate in the law and order auction, the principles of the US, endorsing nil-tolerance policing, 'three strikes' sentencing and minimum sentencing. All thought of rehabilitation in prison has been replaced by the American attitude to social vengeance. So prison life becomes bleaker and more dangerous. Australian academic David Heilpin told the sad story in *Fear or Favour: Sexual Assault of Young Prisoners*. We learn that one in four is raped or sexually brutalised. Yet in India, at least in Tihar, things seem to be different. Perhaps there's something in this Indian experiment that we could look at.

Don't hold your breath.

'At the end of the prison sequence the students come out of the final day of meditation and are embraced and cuddled by the governor. Physical contact is unusual between people of different status, but here there is hugging, tears. Let it be said that it is utterly extraordinary. There is sobbing, there is laughter. Hands are held in a prayerful attitude and then reach out to embrace, cuddle and stroke.'

Sceptics require extraordinary evidence for extraordinary claims. As a sceptic I found Bedi's story compelling — and the images in the Israeli documentary were solid evidence that something extraordinary happened in a terrible place.

13
Suicide in India's Sweden

Conservatives detest Sweden, the paragon of welfare societies, and point to it having 'the highest suicide rate in the world'. This is a furphy, an urban myth. Alcohol is a major problem (hardly surprising when the Swedes spend so much of their time in a dawnless darkness, in the endless night of winter), but their suicide rate is comparatively low. Whereas in Australia the suicide rate is spectacular; it's acknowledged to be the major cause of death among young men. It would be the same with young women, if they chose to use the more emphatic, more masculine methods. In the past women favoured gas. More recently, pills.

In country courts, coroners frequently have open findings on open-and-shut suicide cases, to save families embarrassment. Many a head-on car smash, or cases where cars mysteriously veer into trees, are regarded as accidents when it's painfully clear they were caused by a driver intent on self-destruction. But even after the cooking of the books, Australia's suicide rate is far higher than Sweden's.

I mention suicide because there's an editorial in one of the conservative English-language newspapers headed 'KERALA'S DATE WITH DEATH'. Kerala is, if you like, the Sweden of India, the state that swims against the tide of economic rationalism.

The state that has achieved the highest level of literacy. It is regarded as the world's most successful Communist society.

Yet the headline:

KERALA'S DATE WITH DEATH.

> The Kerala model of development has long been cited at national and international levels as a triumph for rational social engineering. Economists have placed it higher than countries like China on the human development scale. Whether it's high literary levels or low death and birth rates there is a great deal about this state that India can be proud of. But there is one set of statistics that belies the promise inherent in all those positive indicators.

'Positive indicators' — the jargon of the economist rationalist. And note the 'but'. It's a very pleased but.

Now the trumpets blare and a drum roll precedes the triumphant revelation that: 'Kerala has the highest suicide rate amongst all the states in India.'

So much for Marx. So much for the welfare state. So much for literacy and low death and birth rates. At last we can nail the bastards!

> On Wednesday Kerala's Chief Minister, E.K. Nayanar, informed the State Assembly that between April 1992 and March 1997 there were 41,397 cases of suicide in the state. Furthermore, in just two years, between 1996 and 1998, some 15,200 people in the state chose to take their lives. These are just reported cases, the actual number could be much higher.
>
> There cannot be a more damning indictment of Kerala's development paradigm, or its politicians' ability to govern, than these figures. The tragically high number of suicides reflect great human despair and frustration at a mass level. Further, in a region that's justly proud of its medical personnel and facilities the mental wards are full to overflowing.

Why is it so? It's true that Kerala's literacy levels have not been rewarded with outside investment. Consequently there's endemic unemployment and many of the men seek work in the Gulf, leaving women behind to raise the kids on their own. 'Kerala's paradox is the great mismatch between popular expectations and social reality,' purrs the journalist, 'between people's potential and their ability to realise it.'

Isn't it the same all over? Isn't that the paradox of the West where television's blandishments intensify the alienation of people, particularly young people, who are kept out of the picture? The gap between people's potential and their ability to realise it can be Grand Canyonesque. Which is why so many American kids swap their $2-an-hour fast food job to become a gopher for the drug industry. Completely depoliticised, these kids finish up paying cash, coke cash, smack cash, for the Porsches and Mercedes and Rolexes and other brand name dross that others buy on platinum Amex.

India is as violent a country as any, as violent as the USA. Murders are all too common. But tonight the biggest news in the world concerns a massacre in an Arkansas school ground by a couple of kids. No one is pointing the figure at harsh economic conditions. We seem to be dealing with a promiscuous community, with kids whose parents and grandparents can afford to own their own arsenal. Here the blame is being pointed at violent media.

The most astonishing thing about America is how comparatively rare such atrocities are, when you consider the depth of alienation and the pressure of the propaganda, of the pornography of violence. The sex in the Schwarzenneger or Willis movie is sublimated into violence, into phallic projectiles and orgasmic explosions. Given America's long tradition of violence — its wars against the British, the French, the Indian nations, the Cubans, the Mexicans and the civil war that killed well over a million of its own population — it's hard to be surprised by the uncivil wars that rage in the ghettos of the great cities. Given the hideous amusements of the video games, the exultant carnage in the cinema, you can only be astonished at how well behaved these people are most of the time.

And in India? While violent crimes and communal conflicts are all too common, self-murder is rare. A billion people cling to life with desperation and, yes, a dignity that astonishes. Everywhere you go there are people who, judged by Western standards, have no reason to live. But they do live. They endure. Uncomplainingly, stoically.

I remembered the human daddy long-legs I saw begging at the door of a restaurant. I saw a bloke trying to wheel half a tonne of coal 40 kilometres in bloated saddle bags dangling from a pushbike. And each of them live. Endure. There is much in India that is pitiable but there is precious little self-pity.

14

Keepers of the Flame

In pre-dynastic Egypt, people nestled along the Nile the way Australians cling to the coast. Each community had its own animist faith, ascribing mystical qualities to the cat, the hippopotamus, the bull, the jackal, so that every animal had its place, its symbolism. With the passing of time these disparate communities were merged into the kingdoms of Upper and Lower Egypt, to be finally united by the Pharaohs who wore the double crown. Then all the local gods — the animals, the birds, the lions with human heads, the humans with heads of birds — were blended into an all-encompassing theology that necessitated mythologies and theologies that very few, including the high priests, could have claimed to understand. Behold the dynastic menagerie of cow and ibis, of snake and mouse, of crocodile and falcon, of man and beast. To accommodate them all, to fit them into an overarching picture, required the skill of a Rubick, of a creator of cryptic crosswords, but religious hierarchies have always thrived on confusions and contradictions.

Something similar must have happened in India at much the same time. Hinduism is seen as unfolding through successive stages, but many beliefs and practices survive from the beginning, often impervious to the passage of history. Hinduism derives from traditions of the Stone Age inhabitants of India, the Indus Valley civilisation and the Dravidian culture, followed by the

Aryan invasion that led to the religions based on the *Vedas*, which translates as eternal truth.

Elsewhere gods pass their use-by dates, proving themselves as mortal as the men and women who'd believed in them. Thus no one has worshipped the gods of Egypt for 2000 years. Like the gods of the Babylonians, the Etruscans, the Romans, the Greeks and the Norse, the gods have gone to God, gone to ground, gone to graveyards every one. Entire pantheons have fallen silent, broken relics, long lost from living temples appearing, labelled and spotlit, in the dead halls of museums.

But in India the old gods live on. None, it seems, has been dismissed from active service. All have been accommodated and explicated, a space found for them in Hinduism's great jigsaw of faith.

Behold another menagerie of gods in the form of animals, human beings and chimera, gods that morph from form to form, filling the lives of about 80 per cent of India's population — a vast congregation of 800 million people devoted to this or that variation on the theme. There are polytheistic Hindus at one end of the continuum and atheistic Hindus at the other. But for all their differences, they have more in common. Most significantly of all, they are not Muslim.

For the majority of Hindus in India, and for the 30 million Hindus elsewhere in the diaspora, religious life is not so much philosophical or theological as practical, in the sense that certain principles and practices are believed to lead to a better rebirth or even to *Moksa* — the yearning for release from the round of rebirth.

By ordering life according to the principles and practices of Hinduism, or by living it according to particular vows or devotions, by following the map of how to live appropriately, the Hindu hopes to embrace the responsibility and delights of life prior to surrendering to the approach of death.

Not that death is the end. While the Vedas seem ambiguous about the sort of afterlife that Christians might expect, there is a hint, a suggestion that the underlying self or soul persists through the processes of living and dying, and subsists through all the changing appearances of a body. It depends on which holy man you question but consensus seems to have it that, for better or worse, the rebirth continues, at many different levels of appearance, in heavens and hells, in animals or in humans, an ancient process governed by the natural moral law of karma. Finally, if you're lucky, the all but eternal process ends in a sort of fusion that is beyond the power of words to express.

God becomes manifest in many different forms in Hindu India, hence the menagerie that has, over the ages, mocked the scholarly attempts to systematise. But the beliefs seem, in many ways, more profound than the once-upon-a-time, happy (or unhappy) ever after notions of Christianity, with its brief, 6000-year chronology. Hinduism, like science, believes in deep-time, in immense stretches of time, and accepts the notion of creation and destruction.

'Lead me from the unreal to the real; lead me from darkness to light; lead me from death to immortality,' says a prayer of Brhaddaranyaka Upanisad. That, for the majority of Hindus, seems to be the bottom line. But we're dealing with a faith that has mutated, evolved and appropriated for thousands upon thousands of years, until decoding the human gene seems a far simpler task than comprehending this maze of mythology, this fireworks display of faith. To dip into Hinduism is as perilous for a foreigner as dipping into the Ganges, for both contain as many problematic ingredients.

Western scholars argue that 'Hinduism' is a misleading term in that it gives the impression of a unified system of belief and practice. At best it is a convenient shorthand for constituent characteristics of the most complex faith ever invented with, of course, the considerable help of at least fifty centuries.

The Parsis, the keepers of the flame, are far simpler to understand. Their faith is singular, monolithic, as emphatic as the opening chords of Strauss' *Thus Sprach Zarathustra*.

The followers of Zarathustra, the Zoroastrians, decided to leave their Iranian homeland in the eighth century of the Christian era. In the face of increasing Muslim oppression they sought a land where they might enjoy religious freedom. Their migration is described in the *Qissa*, written in 1600 by a Parsi priest, based on oral traditions. It tells how a wise astrologer priest advised the Zoroastrians on when and where they should travel. First came the great Iranian desert, then a journey across the sea. As they approached India a fierce storm blew up and the faithful prayed to be saved, vowing that they would consecrate a major fire, the *Atash Bahram*, as an act of thanksgiving.

On landing safely on Indian soil they approached a local Hindu ruler, Jadi Ranah, seeking permission to settle and consecrate their fire. He questioned them about their beliefs and discovered they shared many values and ideals, such as reverence for the cow and the purity laws. Then he granted them permission, requiring only that they shouldn't carry weapons, should speak the local language and observe its marriage customs.

History records little of the Parsis until the 1700s. However they appear to have lived in peace and gradually spread throughout Jugarat, prospering in trade and textiles. When the Muslim armies invaded the region in the sixteenth century, the Parsis fought alongside the Hindus. They had, after all, little love for the Muslims. But Muslim rule in India proved less harsh than it had been in Iran, and the Parsis continue to flourish.

With the arrival of the European trading powers in the seventeenth century, principally the British, they prospered as middle men in trade, gathering in Mumbai, the city the British had chosen as their base.

They grew rich on overseas trade, establishing businesses in China, East Africa and Britain. The Parsis became the major boat-builders of Mumbai, a profession that was to be crucial to the city's future. They became more and more influential in Mumbai's business — in commerce, banking, industry and above all, the educational institutions of West India. Consequently they grew in political influence and were at the heart of the Indian National Congress from its inception in 1885.

Until the nineteenth century the religion was practised mainly in the home, with worship offered before the household fire. And you still see these household flames today, small flames little larger than the pilot light on a gas heater. But enough to keep the home fires of the faith burning. Trouble is, the employment of non-Parsi servants defiled domestic arrangements — such homes were no longer sufficiently pure to be centres for worship. So although daily prayers were still said at home, the more important acts of worship, or rites of passage, were located in public places — their initiations, weddings, religious feats — leading to a developing hierarchy.

Now, as the century ends, the Parsi community is literally dying. Only in the diaspora are their numbers increasing. So there are more Parsis in Sydney, for example, than in New Delhi or Karachi. The crisis is a topsy-turvy version of the problem of the Jews, whether defined religiously, culturally or racially. Israel is likely to remain the final ghetto while Jews, particularly secular Jews, disappear in the diaspora, marrying out or simply turning their back on traditions. The only demographic that's growing, the only Jewish group exceeding zero population growth, are among the orthodox and ultra-orthodox. But where orthodoxy is the last bastion of Judaism, it is well on the way to destroying the Parsi.

At last count, only 60,000 Parsis survived in all of India. The population is ageing fast and in India, at least, conversion is forbidden, as is marrying out. The demands on the young to marry and have children are clearly counter-productive. 'Populate or perish' has such a catastrophic effect on libido that a high percentage of Parsi men and women will never plight their troth, and those who do marry marry late. And those couples have very few, if any, children.

There's another consequence of procreative propaganda. Young Parsis are over-represented in India's homosexual communities.

I meet a trendy young Parsi, a gay filmmaker, who applied to train in Australia at the National Film Radio and Television School, only to find himself doing media studies at, of all places, Wagga Wagga. Consequently he has few fond memories of Australia; he expresses an intense loathing of every Australian film he's ever seen.

He takes me to an expensive country club in the middle of Mumbai, where tennis courts nestle in gardens of banyan trees and eucalypts. And he sips a G&T on the verandah, with self-effacing servants gliding around us, taking orders in deferential whispers. He makes it clear that his cynicism about Australia extends to India, and that he scorns the epics of Bollywood as much as he does the low-budget, provincial features of Melbourne and Sydney.

He's most interesting when he talks about the future (*sic*) of the Parsi people. Belonging to one of the most influential of the

Parsi families, he'll inherit financial and spiritual responsibilities for one of Mumbai's most important fire temples. It is clearly a responsibility that he will wear lightly, with insouciance, preferring to spend his time in editing rooms or gay clubs. 'And when you're in a gay club in Mumbai, you are surrounded by Parsis,' he says.

So the flame is guttering in the winds of change, but the filmmaker is unconcerned. The great Parsi wealth will have to be divided among the dwindling number of Parsi children. To be born a Parsi, an increasingly rare occurrence, is to be born into a lottery where there are very few tickets and very big prizes.

'I come from Parsi background, which means for most Indians that I am a migrant into what they consider the real India. Of course the migrant communities came here over 1500 years ago, but that is a mere drop in the ocean of Indian time. Secondly, I come from a family that is wealthy, or perceived to be wealthy. We are no longer wealthy but, luckily, perceptions last longer than reality.

'My family is liberal humanist. My grandfather's guru was an English radical whose teachings have permeated down through the generations. So we have a drive for knowledge, a thirst for understanding.

'But I don't think of myself as part of the elite of Mumbai. If anything, I'm part of an international set. I can go anywhere into any country and any society. I am more concerned with the Internet than with elites, with communications than with caste.

'I was in a bar in New York sitting for forty-five minutes next to a man. Finally we got to talking.

'"Where are you from?"

'"From Mumbai."

'"I've never been there but I know someone from Mumbai. Her name is Janet Fine."

'Now Janet Fine happens to be a very close friend of mine. So there we are, in New York, a city of 20 million people. And there I am in Mumbai a city of 40 or 50 million people. And yet we have a friend. This is an experience that happens to me again and again around the world.

'I grew up in Bollywood. I met all the big names and the Big Daddies because they used to come to our dining table and have dinner with us. People from Bollywood are an exaggerated version of Hollywood. They have an exoticism, a certain way of expressing themselves. They work in clichés. And Bollywood, like other film industries, is corrupted, has its mafia. It's a dangerous world. People die.

'A feature film is made in a fragmented way. It's shot over a period of two or three years. The stars have to be dealt with. The egos are enormous. There are many demagogues and demigods. In this situation the filmmaker's soul is destroyed and you become a businessman. But that's not for me. I'm just thirty now and I'll start becoming a businessman when I'm forty. Until then I will do my own thing.'

When he was young he couldn't get away from India fast enough. He rushed to join the diaspora. Now destiny, dynasty, circumstances, pressures have brought him back here. Is he reconcilied to that?

'No, not reconciled. One must always be dissatisfied with the present.'

And he's gay.

'Yes, I'm gay, and I made two documentaries dealing with sexual identity issues, with gay issues in Mumbai. And my directorial feature debut will be a gay film. But I am not a gay filmmaker.'

I seek to reassure him. 'Michelangelo was gay but he's not known as a gay mural painter.'

'Ah, that was a different world! Michelangelo may have had all the beautiful boys but he didn't have to wear the label. Unfortunately I have to wear the label and have none of the beautiful boys. But being gay makes me more of an outsider.

'Of course we're all outsiders on one level or the other. I'm an outsider in India because of all the issues I've mentioned — economics, racial type.'

Blah-blah-blah. The filmmaker praises American cinema, deplores Australian films, Bollywood films and is even contemptuous of Satyajit Ray.

'An example of totalitarian governments exerting their will on the intelligentsia ... his films are quite mundane and boring. The intelligentsia believe that Ray spoke of the real India. He showed poverty, all the wonderful images the West wanted to see. But Indians don't want to see that. We see that on every street corner. So there's no story there. There's no entertainment there.

'Most of my work or portfolio is actually involved with filmmaking. I've done over 200 commercials and several corporate documentaries. All that kind of stuff. I'm media savvy. I know how to sell the India I want to sell to a certain mindset that I want to sell it to.'

Mumbai has been home to a Westernised elite that dictated the culture and policies that dominated India. His family was a member of that Westernised elite. Was English his first language?

'Yes, English. And now, in Mumbai, they're imposing *Marathi* on the masses. Even the name, Mumbai, is *Marathi*. Yet hardly anyone wants to speak it. English is the language of the elites and a Mumbai version of Hindi is the language of the streets. Now we change the name of the city and impose a new language. It's another form of colonialism.

'So I use the language, but use it in an English accent. So I can communicate and distance myself at the same time. It depends on who I'm talking to. For example, if I want some information from a policeman I would put on my best Indian accent or my best *Marathi* accent, because I need his help and want to look humble. But when I'm trying to argue with a taxidriver who's trying to rip me off I'll speak to him in *Marathi* but in a very anglicised accent to let him know that he better not fool around with me.'

Nineteenth-century Parsis pursued Western education with such fervour, and success, that their faith was transformed by it. By studying Western works on Zoroastrianism, frequently written by Protestants, Westernised Parsis reinterpreted their faith in Protestant terms. In reaction, another group of Parsis sought to bolster traditional practices, and found odd partners in theosophy and Madam Blavatsky. So while one group pursued Protestantism, the other recast its beliefs in terms of a Western occult movement. Soon Parsi doctrine had polarised between the liberal Protestants and the orthodox pro-occult factions that shared with Blavatsky ideals of teetotalism, vegetarianism, the doctrine of rebirth, belief in the occult power of prayers (if recited in a sacred language), and in a personal aura. The division continues in the diaspora, principally in America, Canada and Australia, where the faith shows signs of growing. In India there will soon be too few to tend the flame.

I talk to one of the most prominent members of the laity, Khojespie Mistry, in a pleasant apartment, sitting a few yards from the family's sacred lamp. We are surrounded by an ecumenical jumble of sculptures, pictures, fragments of antiquities — an op-shop of cultures, dead civilisations and tourist kitsch. This is the brickiest of brac — a tropical forest of indoor plants, glass cases full of shards of ancient pottery (no pots, just shards) presumably of ancient Aryan or Dravidian origin, and a chaos of furniture styles. Like me, my host has a hatred for uncluttered surfaces and sees every piece of blank wall as a vacuum that, naturally, needs to be filled. So here's a lurid painting of Christ over a glitzy Thai airport Buddha and, nearby, a tizzy ceramic mask of Tutenkhamen. Is the host a syncretist? Is he making a statement about the equivalence of religions or the many paths to God?

Let there be no doubt, however, that the room is dominated by the naked flame, burning in a lamp suspended on chains in the corner of the room. Not so much a chip off the old block as a flicker from the great flame that we'll be visiting that afternoon, the Zoroastrian counterpart to the Olympic flame that ignited the torches that have, over the years, led to Berlin, Rome, Melbourne, Los Angeles, Barcelona and New Orleans. A direct relation to the eternal flames that glow inside or outside a thousand war memorials.

Mistry is a tall man, as theatrically dignified as the maitre'd of an expensive restaurant. His reputation precedes him: he is a major figure in the community and, though a lay person, sees himself as a considerable scholar of his faith. Indeed his hospitality will only cool when he learns that I am to visit the high priest at an important temple. In a few well-chosen words, superficially respectful, he manages to dismiss him as a spiritual mediocrity, a theological also-ran. 'Yes, a very fine man. Really quite knowledgable. Yes, quite knowledgable.'

In the course of our conversation his wife and teenage children enter quietly, are introduced with fond condescension and dismissed. Indeed, he takes time off from being dismissive about the notion of females in the priesthood to dismiss his wife, though she, herself, is a significant figure in both the community and her profession.

It emerges that the principal reason he agreed to the interview was because of a highly critical story in the religious section of *Time* magazine, in which his branch of the Mumbai Parsi community is criticised for its conservatism — an uncompromising view of the faith that is accelerating its demise. When he asks me whether I've read the magazine I decide that a fib is required. 'No, I haven't.'

'Dreadful, dreadful. Appallingly ill-informed.' And he makes it clear that I'll be properly briefed. Do I wish to take notes?

'No, thank you.' I gesture towards the tape recorder.

Addressing the microphone he is more theatrical. I'd hoped for a conversation but, instead, get a performance.

He disputed the gloomy demographic reports. 'As far as India's concerned, I think our numbers peaked at about 110,000, thirty or forty years ago. But then the entire community lived in India. Today, thirty years hence, we have a lot of Parsis migrating to the United States, to Canada, to Australia and a community of settled Zoroastrians in England as well. If you look at the global figure I think you will find the numbers haven't substantially diminished. But this bogey of diminishing numbers is constantly resurrected, because if you go on telling the community that our numbers are diminishing then more and more people are going to say, "Well, let's open our doors to conversion." So it's a political ploy.

'Yes, there have been pressures from time to time for Zoroastrians to accept converts. But think of the plus side of not accepting them. My people, in the name of religion, have never killed people. Generally when conversion is promoted or encouraged, there is an immense amount of bloodshed, because there's a presupposition that one religion is better than another. We believe that if God is one, then God in his wisdom has placed different people in different religions, and who are we to decide as to which religion we should be part of? In a sense, it's religious tolerance on our part which prevents us from trying to market our religion as being the religion for the world.'

He then disputes the usual history of the faith 'No, it didn't begin in the sixth or seventh century BC. Today most serious scholars put the date back between 1200 and 1500 BC, which makes Zoroastrianism the oldest revealed religion in the world. Very many factors and a lot of scholarship has gone into this dating question. Archaeological evidence is now emerging from Afghanistan, Tadzhikistan and those areas. While we don't have definitive conclusive proof that Zarathustra lived in 1500 BC, the scholars are now pushing his date back. That sixth-century debate was suggested by Western scholars because it was convenient — they wanted Zarathustra to fit in to the time when Confucius was born and when the Buddha was born.'

I suggested to Mistry that the Parsis had flourished in Mumbai because they'd been the go-betweens, to some extent the collaborators with the Raj. He disputed this interpretation, pointing out that Parsis had been among India's most prominent freedom fighters. In any case, all Indians had had to come to terms with the British who were, after all, in India for 200 years.

'Had it not been for Parsi money and Parsi foresight, Mahatma Gandhi would not have been sent to South Africa from India to champion the freedom cause.'

Was the Parsi community resented because of its economic dominance?

'I don't believe that we're resented at all. One of the beauties of living in India is that India is a mosaic of religions, a place where every religion has been allowed to flower. Personally I have never detected a sense of resentment. If anything we have the most amazing respect which is given to us by all the communities because, at the end of the day, our religion promotes life as a celebration.'

We're talking in a room full of fragments of other cultures and other times. In this country Zoroastrians are but a small tile in the Indian mosaic. Given the sectarian conflicts of India there must be abrasions between the Hindus, the Muslims and the Sikhs and the Parsis?

'I think we're the most fortunate community in India because there are no abrasions. We live in a very tolerant way. The host communities treat us with immense respect. And because we do not share our religion, we do not seek converts, no community feels threatened by us.'

I question him about including Christian, Islamic and Buddhist works in his collection.

'Images of many faiths. But they are here purely from an artistic point of view. I hasten to stress that as Zoroastrians we do not promote icon worship. So what you see by way of religious statues are simply artistic expressions. Nor would I want you to think that Zoroastrians are eclectic by way of belief. We are not.

'Nor are we a dogmatic faith. Zarathustra promotes the supremacy of wisdom — the use of your own mind. We are not a proscriptive faith. Modern management could do well to listen to the words of Zarathustra. He said, "Reflect with your ears to the best things: reflect with a clear mind, man by man for himself." In other words: listen, think and then act. Consider that those words were uttered three and a half thousand years ago and you begin to realise the strength of the faith. Another is that we believe that evil does not come from good. We believe that evil is antithetical to the good and therefore pain, misery, suffering and, indeed, death are all seen to be the temporary triumphs of evil and not the work of God.'

I ask him to talk about death. Does he believe in an afterlife?

'We believe that every thought, word and deed that we generate in this life is recorded at the end of our life, where our soul is self-judged at what we symbolically call the Bridge of the Separated. At the so-called bridge the soul, if it has generated more good thoughts, words and deeds than bad thoughts, words and deeds, it is automatically drawn into the House of Song, which later Christianity would call Heaven.'

While my host is undoubtedly charming, he is also pompous. Everything is said with ponderous certainty and pedantic emphasis. Whether he's declaiming aspects of the faith, or describing the universal respect in which his community is held, he uses a voice that will brook no argument.

The idea of self-judgment reminds me of the ancient Egyptian belief in Maat. Instead of a bridge to be crossed there's a pair of scales on which your heart is to be weighed. And if your wrong-doing has made it heavier than a feather, you will not be saved. Fortunately the hieroglyphs suggest that most hearts passed the test.

'Yes, there are similarities with Egypt. But as I understand it they do not go into the precise details of the thought, the word and the action. Zoroastrianism is extremely precise. And therefore we are masters of our own destiny. We cannot blame fate, for example. We cannot resort to the notion of a previous life. If I do something right, I reward myself for it in the afterlife. If I do something wrong in this physical existence, I punish myself.'

And what happens to a condemned soul?

'Well, if a soul has generated more bad thoughts, words and deeds in this existence, it relegates itself to hell, to the House of Deceit. And it will remain there until the end of time. But note this: unlike Christianity we do not have the concept of eternal damnation. We believe that there is an end of time, a time when evil will be rejected by man, God's finest creation. So we believe that all the souls will be resurrected from the House of Deceit, as well as from the House of Song. This means that even the wickedest person in the world will, at the end of time, when time ceases to exist, be resurrected. Ours is a very optimistic doctrine.'

Thus good triumphs over evil. I ask if he's seen much evidence of this happy outcome in the century we're about to leave.

'I think there is immense evidence to suggest that good is triumphing over evil. I think that most of us are victims of the media, if you'll forgive me. So, for example, if something bad happens the media reports it. But if something good happens it is seldom reported. So if somebody bonks an old lady crossing the streets, then that's news. But if that old lady is helped across the street by a young lad, it's not news.

'Think about this century versus the last. Today there is more education in the world. There are more hospitals in the world. There is more food in the world. So, from the Zoroastrian point of view, the world is qualitatively improving. Death is not seen as the work of God. Finally evil will be defeated. Evil is parasitic to the good. Here is some imagery I'd like to suggest: we have light and light is god. If you move away from light, darkness emerges. But you can't say darkness comes from light. You *can* say darkness is the absence of light. So evil is an absence of good. And on its own, it can't exist. In other words, evil only comes into being where there is something positive which God has made. Therefore, because there is life, there can be death, but there cannot be death before life.'

He has raised the notion of light as goodness. Let us now extrapolate from that into the importance of fire in Parsi ritual.

'As Zoroastrians we believe in the greatness of the seven creations. We believe that the Lord of Wisdom fashioned the seven creations of the skies, water, earth, plant, cattle, man and fire. Fire is the seventh creation, so we believe that a consecrated fire is the actual force of God. I would suggest to you that a consecrated fire may be likened to Jesus Christ and Christianity. Just as Jesus is seen as the Son of God, we see a consecrated fire as the Son of God as well, but with an important difference. Our consecrated fire has to be looked after, has to be tended carefully by the priest, is fed aromatic wood five times a day. Whereas the Christian cross you can leave unattended.'

I ask about the funeral arrangements. Why is there is no burning of the dead?

'There was a tradition of burial among some of the kings in ancient times. But we have never burnt our dead. The method we use is the Tower of Silence, or the exposure method, which once again fits beautifully into our theology. Because death is the work of evil, we don't believe in polluting the elements. We don't believe in polluting the earth or the waters. And the only unlimited creation that exists is the sky.

'If we burn our dead we would desecrate fire. If we drown our dead we are sullying the water. So we became the first religion in the world to preach what modern man calls ecology. Our method of disposal is excellent. We do not waste natural resources. For example, if we burnt our dead we would be using electricity, which is a scarce commodity. If we buried our dead we would be wasting vast tracts of land. If anything we should be complimented on the Towers of Silence. Here in the city of Mumbai, indeed in the poshest part of Mumbai, namely Malibar Hill, you find our tower. We have given Mumbai a living lung.'

And the bodies are cleansed by birds, by vultures?

'The process may sound horrific initially, but it's very hygienic and quite scientific. The vultures gobble a body in a matter of a few hours. The remaining bones are allowed to stay in this Roman-like amphitheatre for thirty days. The bones are swept into a central pit where they eventually turn into a fine powder. It is excellent economically and, most importantly, it's egalitarian. Whether you're rich or whether you're poor, the disposal is exactly the same. Unlike Christianity where, if you are rich you can have a stone mausoleum built over your tomb. Or if you're a rich Hindu your body could be cremated in pure sandalwood. As far as Zoroastrianism is concerned there is complete equality when a person dies.'

I ask about equality between men and women in the faith.

'Considering the antiquity of our religion we have the most amazing concept of equality. But we have to recognise that equality operates at different levels. Clearly there isn't physical equality in terms of sheer strength between men and women. But at a spiritual level both the souls of man and woman are judged in exactly the same way. So there is equality in death, equality in the spiritual world. And even in this world, in his celebrated hymn, in his last hymn, Zarathustra says:

Listen ye brides and ye bridegrooms.
May your marriage be based on truth.
For it should be of good gain to each.

'For a man to have preached this three and a half thousand years ago says, I think, a lot.'

Can women join the priesthood?

'Women do not join the priesthood because we have strict laws of purity. Most religions subscribe to the idea that menstruation is ritually impure, ritually dirty. From that point of view, if we encouraged women to be priests it would be very difficult to maintain the laws of purity, because it takes sixteen days before a person can be ritually pure. Man or woman. And if one suffers from ritual impurity — and I stress it's ritual, I'm not saying that it's biological impurity because menstruation is clearly essential ...'

I agree that this is a persuasive belief, common to Hindus and to Hassidic Jews, for example.

I leave the rich man's apartment, where the religious art is not to be confused with the religion, and cross the city to where

Dasturje Kotwal, a high priest, a *dastur*, lives in a gloomy apartment in a battered building. The apartment is dark but he is very bright with his white beard, bright teeth, white cap. Like Mistry, he likes to surround himself with odd, unconnected things. Only some of them linger in the memory. A huge, dark bookcase with only a few dozen books — most notably, a 1930s volume, in fake leather binding, called A *Treasury of Detective Stories*. A bad print, in a dilapidated frame, of an English cottage garden. And, of all things, a large plaster statue of the Air India Maharaja. Kotwal's English was thickly accented, difficult to understand, but he yearned to communicate. One imagined him stern and unyielding with his congregation but with me he was wistful, appealing.

He restates the official history of the faith, his chronology conflicting with the lay scholar's. Zoroastrianism is one of the oldest surviving religions and was founded in Persia by Zarathustra in the sixth or seventh century BC. Zarathustra was born Mazar-I-Sharif in what is now Afghanistan, and at one time his influence stretched from India to the Mediterranean. In India his followers are known as Parsis, which derives from the Persians, and their religion was one of the first to postulate an omnipotent and invisible god: a god of light who is symbolised by fire.

When he tells me that he's the keeper of a flame that's been burning for over a thousand years I can't help but feel sceptical. Surely there must have been times when someone fell asleep on the job or there was a downpour through a leaking roof. A time when the flame was extinguished and had to be furtively rekindled, with a little help from a can of kero and a Bic. After all, it's happened in the relay race of the Olympic torch.

I realise that I will not be allowed into the temple so I ask the priest to tell me about the fire inside.

'The final fire is in a simple square room. There the fire is enthroned in a beautiful silver fire vase. And the fire that burns is made of different fires. For example, in Udvarda, 200 kilometres north of Mumbai, we have the oldest fire in India, just over a thousand years old. All in all, we have eight such cathedral fires ... and each has been made of sixteen different fires including the fire of lightning, which has to be witnessed by two Zoroastrians.

When that lightning occurs, when it strikes the earth, those burning embers have to be preserved so that, in the future, the fire can be used and purified to kindle a cathedral fire.

'In order to consecrate the sacred fire we have to collect sixteen types of fire, sift them, purify them, consecrate them, collate them, and install the fire which has become a living entity into the sanctum sanctorum. And there it can burn for a thousand years or more.'

I ask about the other sources of fire.

DK: There is the corpse-burning fire. It is a fire sullied through contact with dead matter. Now this fire has been injured and harmed. It has been harassed immensely. You must collect it and make the spirit of the fire happy. We take fire from the corpse-burning fire, from the fire of a tinner, of a goldsmith, of a blacksmith. We take fire from the head of a family.

PA: And the fire of war?

DK: Yes, we take that fire. And the fire of caravans because in ancient times caravans were going from one place to another, from one country to another.

PA: So you have to heal the fire?

DK: Yes.

PA: So some fires are sick or dying?

DK: Oh yes. So it is a meritorious act to collect all the fires and consecrate them into one.

I congratulate him on a very poetic religion. You are, I say, a poet of fire. And I ask him if it's true that Parsis do not smoke because smoking trivialises fire.

DK: Yes, because you should not put anything into your mouth that is burning. It is a sin, because it is something very holy and sacred. Our feelings are hurt.

PA: What of the fire that's used for cooking?

DK: Fire is sacred to us. Yet there are fires that can be used for lowly purposes.

PA: Are there dietary prohibitions?

DK: According to our religion there is no prohibition. It is only because of our association with our brother communities like the Muslims and the Hindus that our people are not eating pork or beef.

PA: What is the attitude of the Zoroastrians to science?

DK: Zoroastrianism is happiness within. It is harmony in the environment. Then, clearly, science is an aid to us. What do I mean by that? Science deals with empirical reality whereas religion goes beyond, into the spiritual dimension. So a good Zoroastrian can be a good scientist. You see, our religion leads itself to the polishing of the mind, to the use of the mind. Which can bring you to science or medicine or law.

Our theology deals with evolution in a very logical way. Our theology says that the first creation was the sky, the next was the waters, then the earth and the plants, the animals, the man and fire. Think of it. Science tells us that first there were gasses then liquids then solids then plant life and eventually animal life. So everything meshes beautifully. Clearly when one has a creation story, as every religion does, that story may not lend itself fully to Darwin's theory. Nonetheless I say that Zoroastrianism is a wonderful religion absolutely in sync with the twentieth century. In fact, we're totally ready to move into the twenty-first century because, for us, work is worship, life is a celebration, and we as Zoroastrians have to promote happiness wherever we go.

My parents and relatives were not very happy about my taking the priesthood. The priesthood is not a rich profession. But it came from within. You have to sacrifice everything.

In the Parsi community there are two classes: the laity and the clergy. Priesthood and the priestly class is hereditary. So a member of the laity, even one who becomes a distinguished scholar, someone who succeeds in business, may not be a priest.

Both of us have someone in mind.

DK: No, he would not be initiated into the priesthood. The priest has to be initiated after being trained in a seminary, after learning by heart many chapters of the sacred texts, and he must be proficient in performing rituals.

PA: How long has the family been in the business?

DK: Since the twelfth century.

PA: That is before the Parsis came to India.

DK: Yes. I can remember the names of thirty ancestors. And there were others before them. But I do not know the names.

PA: And all of them men?

DK: There are references, faint references, in the texts to a woman helping her husband in the task of tending the fire. Perhaps some other functions. So women may have had a place in the priesthood in ancient Iran. But as far as India is concerned? No. Yet the woman is on a par with the man. She is not below him. Zarathustra himself, thousands of years ago, visualised and praised the woman who is faithful to her husband, who is well instructed in religion.

PA: When are you initiated into the priesthood?

DK: Before puberty. The initiation takes about a month. The candidate has to undergo purificatory baths, each of ten days, when he has to bathe four or five times a day. And when he goes to bed it is essential that he shouldn't have nocturnal pollution.

I make a note of that: no nocturnal pollution. Now I turn the conversation to conversion.

PA: Why do you not convert people?

DK: But I do. I daily convert people. I bring the laity to the light from darkness. If they are on the wrong path I bring them to the enlightened path. For us this is conversion. Conversion does not mean you forsake your religion and adopt another.

PA: Yet in America there are splinter groups who are going out and seeking converts.

DK: Yes, but these people do everything for money. They make religion into a business. This is not a religion. This is a travesty of religion.

The priest belongs to an oral tradition of worship. Beneath the white hat is a great memory of ritual.

DK: Yes, I have learnt many books by heart.

PA: What about death?

DK: Death is a transformation. A man is made of physical and spiritual parts. His guiding spirit, intellect, consciousness, these are all spiritual parts. Bones, blood, body, flesh ... these are physical parts. Death is the separation of the spiritual from the physical.

PA: Yet the faith believes in resurrection of the body — a concept that influenced the Judaeo-Christian tradition.

DK: Yes, resurrection of the body. Exactly. Judaism, Christianity and Islam were all influenced by Zoroastrianism in matters of escatology.

PA: And what about the death of the faith?

DK: I am not concerned. You see, youngsters are becoming more aware of religion. They want to learn. They want to be enlightened. They say why this, why that. They do not want to accept, do this, do that. But they will obey once you have taught them.

PA: Yet there are fewer and fewer to obey. Is this not a great tragedy?

> DK: No. We came here in a few boats and we multiplied. We preserved our religion and our race. We preserved our exclusivity.

I mention the name of the lay scholar. Now the high priest is in high dudgeon.

> DK: Our priestly organisation should be stronger. But everyone thinks that he, himself, is a high priest. Everyone thinks he can do whatever he likes. The laity challenges the authority of the priesthood, even in the newspapers. They write against me very often and, because I tell the truth, because I say what is, because I am not afraid of anyone, because I am faithful to my religion, I displease them. But that is not my problem. That is his problem.
>
> PA: Do you have children and grandchildren to carry on the task?
>
> DK: No, nobody is going to carry on anything. Because they have no aptitude like myself. I have two sons and a daughter. The eldest is twenty-five and the youngest child, my daughter, is twenty-one. They are all working in offices.
>
> PA: And none of them has the calling?
>
> DK: No.

Behind him, pinned to the wall, is an elaborate Hindu image. I ask a question with my finger. He shakes his head. 'It is only a calendar.' The blaze of anger has passed and he is once again a cheerful man, a happy man.

> DK: Yes, and my cheerfulness comes from God. And the sacred fire.
>
> PA: It's said that you're also a stern man.
>
> DK: Yes, I am stern. But I am very kind-hearted. I seem stern because I am steadfast and I say what I believe. And I am angry with some members of the community who care too much for money.

We agree that Mammon is a powerful god.

Finally I ask him to sing. He has a reputation as a fine singer. Would he sing a prayer?

Delighted by the invitation, he opens the old bookcase and pulls out a volume of prayers from beside the treasury of detective stories. He opens it and begins to sing, an immensely long prayer, in a high, strong voice. His fingers trace the words as he sings, but he doesn't seem to be reading. So I take the book from his hands, with a smile, and close it. He smiles back as he sings because, it's true, he doesn't need the book. He knows all the prayers off by heart, countless thousands of them.

As we leave his office I can see his family sprawled in front of a TV set up in the next room. 'That is my son,' he says, quite proudly, of a young man sprawled in an armchair, staring at *Mr Ed* dubbed into Hindi. He shakes his head. 'No, no, he does not have the calling.'

15

The Homogenisation of India

Back in 1991 there was only state-owned television. Now there is an endless number of channels, and the air is thick with their cables. As a consequence the Indian middle class is now coming into contact with an international consumer culture. And Indian culture is trying to catch up.

Considered India's leading cultural theorist, Partha Chattergee, an historian for the Centre for Studies of Social Sciences (who also teaches at the Anthropology Department at Columbia University in New York), was happy to chat about his nation's chattering classes.

He spoke with some regret that Calcutta had lost its significance as a film production centre, moving to Mumbai and Madras. At the same time, most major films involve foreign locations — setting scenes in the West to emphasise cultural and life-style comparisons. Indian film producers are now seeking export markets. They're now aimed at the many millions of Indians in the diaspora, and made with audiences in the Middle East and Africa in mind. Again, cultural compromises are the order of the day.

As well, films are marketed through film clips — placing an increasing emphasis on music. While music has always been an important aspect of the film industry, now it is absolutely crucial.

If the music video is a success, the film is almost certain to be a success. If it fails, the film flops.

The homogenisation seen in cinema is echoed throughout society, so even a major religious festival can now be sponsored by a US corporation such as Coca-Cola. There is also the homogenisation of clothing and food. Twenty years ago there were clear regional distinctions, but with the advent of national media and the growing influence of advertising, a uniform taste is being created so that no matter where you travel you'll see the same fashions and eat the same meals.

Does this mean that regional loyalties are being replaced by a newly emergent national identity? He thought not. India was moving towards an international identity.

Communism in India

We'd booked a chat with the mellifluously entitled Mr E.M. Chankaran Namboodiripad who'd presided over the Indian Communist movement for five decades, but he elected to join Karl, Freidrich, Vladimir, Josef and Mao while we were waiting for the taxi. A Marxist till the end, he refused to let them take him to the hospital — he was suffering breathing problems caused by pneumonia — until he'd completed his weekly column for the 'party organ'. That's what the Communist Party always had — not newspapers but party organs. But Namboodiripad's own party organs were beyond repair, or the help of a party organ transplant. Having filed his copy, he suffered two cardiac arrests in rapid succession.

So I head for the Centre for Policy Research instead, a think tank where I meet Rajmohan Gandhi, a calm and impressive gentleman whose authority derives from being the Mahatma's grandson. (Prominent in moral rearmament, he was briefly guru to the young Kim Beazley.) Beside him sits Ved Marwah, a big wheel in policing, internal security and other forms of crowd control, and an ex-minister, K.C. Sivaramakrishnan, who headed the Department of Urban Developments.

We discuss the death of the grand old man of Indian Marxism and I ask about the power of communism in contemporary India. Communists rule in three states: Kerala, West Bengal and Tripura, on the other side of Bangladesh. Elsewhere, despite the immense poverty, the Communist Party seems at death's door. But the consensus is that it's merely dormant and although a full-scale eruption seems unlikely, it could start hissing and spluttering at any moment.

We then ask ourselves why India's role in the wider world, nuclear bombs notwithstanding, seems so marginal. After all, India has been flavour of the month ever since Dickie Attenborough's film on Rajmohan's grandpa. Those at the table were clearly miffed by the off-Broadway status of their great nation which they saw, to some extent, as a consequence of the world adjusting from a bipolar to a tripolar model. 'Because of this it may take some time to accommodate India.' It's clear they look back to the era of Indira Gandhi, when India cast itself in the role of head of the non-aligned nations as a golden age.

I express surprise that, since my last trip, the amount of international news in the major Indian newspapers seems to have dramatically diminished. Is this symptomatic of India becoming isolationist, inward looking?

'Perhaps it is. But then, we have so many internal problems. We are looking to find a new role. We are a nation in waiting.'

Ideas and issues circle the table and, over tea and bickies, I ask whether this was a time for Indians to feel proud. A silence falls. They consider. Finally Rajmohan fields the question which, it is clear, he finds the most interesting one of the session.

'Yes, but the feeling of pride is deep within. You have to search for it.'

'Even at the time of the fiftieth anniversary?'

'Even then. Particularly then. For we have not solved our problems. And for most people life is very, very hard. There is not a lot of energy left over with which to feel pride.'

'We do not mass-market pride here, as in the US, where national pre-eminence is both a truth and a consensus,' said Ved Marwah.

Gandhi wanted to see India as a powerful, spiritual presence in South East Asia. 'I'm a utopian,' he beams.

It is a view I often hear expressed — a sense that India's destiny involves being a guru-nation as well as an economic and political force.

'I'm a utopian.' In that case, Ved Marwah has much in common with Australians who have a long history of pursuing utopias. I told them of Australians rushing off into jungle clearings in the hope of creating perfect societies. These days, however, the mass of the population want the utopia they glimpse on the telly, the one that lives in the fabled Land of the Ad.

They smiled. That utopia is one that is now becoming all too familiar to Indians.

The Movies

The world was astonished when one of the least dazzling of Hollywood stars became president. And once Ronald Reagan had completed his journey from Rodeo Drive to Pennsylvania Avenue, from bad scripts to the Inaugural Address, what seemed truly odd was that it was him — rather than a more obvious movie star contender such as Jimmy Stewart who, as Frank Capra's Everyman, had gone to Washington in the 1930s, or Henry Fonda who, as the embodiment of liberalism, had portrayed everyone from Tom Joad to the recalcitrant juror in *Twelve Angry Men*, not to mention at least one president in a film about a nuclear crisis — who'd won the most coveted role in the country.

Then, of course, there was John Wayne, the Mount Rushmore memorial on two legs, more an embodiment of America's belief in itself than any politician could hope to be. Over a decade after his death he is still, according to some surveys, the most admired actor in the entire pantheon. Had this icon in a Stetson, in a green beret, ever run for office he'd have been a shoo in.

It's not only in America that the actor has become an actor on the political stage. The Philippines recently elected a thespian as President, while any number of soapie stars have been exalted by the electorate in Central and South America. Nonetheless it's in India where one thing leads to another.

In India, the cinema still holds the role it enjoyed in the wider world in the 1930s, offering the working class, for a modest investment, a technicolor dreaming. It's at the movies that the ordinary, illiterate Indian can see the sacred texts brought to life. It's in India that the blurring between fact and fiction, between religion and entertainment, can entirely confuse the issue, elevating the actors beyond mere politics into the pantheon of the deities.

I find a novel in a bookshop in Mumbai — *Showbusiness*, by Shashi Tharoor, author of *The Great Indian Novel*, a book I'd enjoyed years earlier. A child of the Indian diaspora, born in London and raised in Mumbai, Calcutta and Delhi, Tharoor has worked for the UN for the last twenty years. His novel on Bollywood, on the Mumbai film industry, is more than a fine piece of satire. It represents a considerable contribution to anthropological literature.

Bollywood is notoriously corrupt, a realm of gangsters. Mind you, Hollywood may present a more reputable facade but it, too, is rotten to the core, as much involved in laundering of gangsters' money as are the casinos in Las Vegas. The studios are the other casinos, and Los Angeles, rather than Vegas, provides the biggest gaming room on Earth.

And if film industries are traditionally attractive to gangsters, they are also beloved of politicians. After all, the two professions depend on fleeting, evanescent images, on contrived dramatics and shallow histrionics. It's a moot point whether cinema or politics is the most intent on providing photo opportunities.

Shashi Tharoor looks at Bollywood in terms of its gangster connections and political influence. He tells the story of the rise, rise and calamitous fall of Ashock Banjara, product of the finest public school in independent India, secretary of the Shakespeare Society at St Francis College, no less, not to mention son of the Minister of State for Minor Textiles. The book begins with him:

> ... chasing an ageing actress around a papier-mâché tree in an artificial drizzle, lip-synching to the tinny inanities of an aspiring (and highly aspirating) playback singer. But it *is* me, it's my mouth that's moving in soundless ardour, it's my arms that are gesticulating under the shawl that's draped toga-style over my khadi-kurta, it's my voice calling for social justice, rural development, and votes.

But he lives to find himself marginalised — his fame cynically exploited by the ruling party.

> Me, Ashock Banjara, superstar of the silver screen, heart-throb of the misty-eyed masses, unchallenged hero of every scene in which I've been called upon to play a part, languishing in the back rows of the House of the People, the Lok Sabha, while cretinous netas in crumpled khadi, their eyes and waistlines bulging, hold forth inarticulately on the irrelevent ... As I take in the spectacle of representative democracy in action and yawn. Ashock Banjara, parliamentary acolyte, ignored and condescended to by people who wouldn't be cast as second villains in Bollywood: what is life coming to? I thought they'd at least make me a Minister. After all, I was better known and more widely recognised than everyone bar the Prime Minister.

Take the cult of M.G. Ramachandran, usually known as MGR. The film star became Tamil Nadu's chief minister and mentor to the extraordinary 'walking goddess' Jayaram Jayalalitha. MGR was so adored by the multitudes, who'd completely confused the actor with his transcendental roles, that scores committed suicide by jumping out of trains, or by self-immolation, when he died about ten years ago.

Then there is someone like N.T. Rama Rao in Andhra, who's played so many gods in mythological epics that people have built a temple to him. Or the actor in Madras who has defeated the forces of injustice and evil in so many films that the masses are pleading with him to take over the state government and set everything right.

More modestly, actors in the West are content to identify themselves with political movements, Marilyn Monroe singing 'Happy Birthday' to Jack Kennedy, Barbra Streisand leading the pack for Clinton, and Richard Gere coming out for the Dalai Llama and Tibet. That way they can have their clout and eat their cake too — given that a movie star still out-grosses the most successful of politicians, even a president.

Indian films flood out, with their political consequences. Thus far the energy level remains high enough to deflect the invasions of Hollywood though the prow of the *Titanic* seemed to carve the same, wide swathe here as it did in every nook and cranny of the planet.

Tharoor describes the illiterate villagers who go six or seven times to the same film, and who think the actors are the heroes they play. 'The rural masses don't make fine distinctions between the actor and the part ... that's why children aren't being named Pranay any more, or Prem Chopra, because the actors' own real names are so completely identified with their screen villainy.'

At the height of political potency, Ashock inadvertently pushes his own father from the political pedestal, a man who has paid and overpaid his dues to Congress. His lifetime of struggle, his attempts to climb the ladder, are mocked by his son's ascendency.

> I'll try and explain myself to you, Ashock, to describe the gulf I felt between our world. My India is periodically torn apart in outbursts of communal and sectarian violence; but communal awareness only enters your films if the producer wants to obtain an entertainment-tax waiver for 'promoting national integration'. Every hero, and for that matter every villain, is casteless and unplaceable ... whereas in my India you'll never get anywhere with a man without knowing who he is, where he comes from, what his caste affiliations are. (In my constituency a man's surname alone can frequently tell you which way he will vote, but in your films hardly anyone of consequence in the script has a surname.) In my India poverty means distended bellies and eyes without hope, whereas in your films the poor change costumes for each verse of their songs and always have enough strength to beat up the villains. In your films evil is easily personalised ... but in my India I see that evil pervades an entire social and economic system that your films do nothing to challenge, a system that indeed places the likes of your own producers amongst the grubby cluster at its pyramid ... And yet I suppose our worlds are not all that far apart. You function amid fantasies, playing your assigned role in a make-believe India that has never existed and can never exist. As a politician I too play a role in a world of make-believe, a world in which I pretend that the ideas and principles and values that brought me to politics can still make a difference. Perhaps I too am performing, Ashock, in an India that has never really existed and can never exist.

The old man describes a world where politicians make speeches in which they pretend their actions and positions are motivated by policy, principle, ideology, the interests of their constituents and their vision of India. In reality issues and values determine little.

> They win on caste calculations, they get money for suborning laws they have enthusiastically passed, they switch parties and abandon platforms at the dangling of a lucrative post or a ministerial birth. And yet why should anyone be surprised? Politics is the art of the expedient: no politician can afford to look beyond the next election and the means that will help him win it. Politics is an end in itself, just like the Hindi film. You cannot judge either by external standards.

In Australia, the voters are agog when Senator Colston defects from the ALP, or Cheryl Kernot from the Democrats. In India, such defections are a daily occurrence. Political parties wax and wane as their leaders exhort them or abandon them. In India a party political affiliation is no more substantial than a role in a movie. The script changes and suddenly you're in a new costume, declaiming new lines of dialogue. The Indian politician is ideologically promiscuous, always ready to be seduced by a more seductive offer.

When I visit the shrine to Mahatma Gandhi I find a number of long-term protesters sitting surrounded by placards at the gate, seeking signatures for the petitions. One is a Tibetan, protesting Delhi's ambivalence to the Chinese occupation. Another protests the constant defections from this party or that; his placards demanding legislation to prevent it. I sit on the ground beside him and listen to his impassioned complaint about duplicity and disloyalty. In Australia, to cross the floor is still seen as an act of treason. In India, as much traffic crosses the floor as crosses the Gandhi Ghat car park.

The gap Tharoor describes between political rhetoric and political performance couldn't be greater. While Indian politics abounds with Graham Richardsons, few pollies have the brutal candour of the NSW rights' erstwhile fixer. The colloquial directness that characterises so much of the political debate in

Canberra, or in Spring or Macquarie streets, is unheard of in a country where the lowest manoeuvres must be couched in the noblest, most grandiloquent language. The more you hear of it the less you trust it. You quickly get to the point where the loftier the language the more sceptical your response.

Ashock Banjara's father rises steadily, if unspectacularly, up the ladder. He holds state office, then national portfolios as Deputy Minister and as a Minister of State. But Cabinet eludes him, as did the important portfolios — 'Instead I've gone from party hack to party elder statesman without the usual intervening phase of senior government responsibility'. He had hoped to hand on his mantle to his other son, Pranay, who has been learning the ropes. But Ashock's rise seems irresistible.

Everywhere in India you find yourself buying smuggled goods. You need a filter for your Nikon? Sorry, Nikons are not an approved brand. But every street hawker will sell you a Nikon, a lens hood, one that's been brought in from Dubai. Ashock's father describes the system:

> In that country even challenging a vested interest becomes a vested interested. So smugglers are anti-national? Very well, but Bombay's most successful smuggler is avidly sought after for campaign contributions by every party, including mine, and his endorsement is highly valued for the block of votes he delivers from his community. So basically the same class of people pass the protectionist laws, get support from both the beneficiaries and the violators of these laws at election time, buy goods from the smugglers, and then denounce them in their films.

He tells Prime Minister Gandhi that 'we'd solve half the crime in this country by not passing laws that everyone felt it necessary to break. She looked down her patrician nose at me in that way she has.' And he does not get his promotion.

Given that Bollywood is as central to an understanding of Indian culture as Hollywood is to America and, tragically, our own, I watch as many films as I can — formulaic, full of music, melodrama and mythology. And I find that the video clips mark a forward or backward step, depending on your point of view.

Here the traditional images described by Tharoor are being hybridised, Western influences incorporated.

The most characteristic scenes involve, as usual, lovers running at each other in slow motion, singing their heads off, their lip movements wildly out of sync with the recorded duets performed by others. What makes them different is that as they run at each other their costumes change, as do the settings. One moment they'll be running along the steps of a *ghat*. The next through a municipal park. Then they'll be rapidly approaching each other in the vicinity of a temple or on the street at night. And as they run towards each other her sari will become a leather mini or a pair of very tight slacks. Or even a tu-tu. But she will remain, in essence, the shy, virginal Indian heroine of tradition.

He, in contrast, is the Fonz on steroids. Brylcreem is alive and well and living in India — in thick, busby-like hairdos. The cinema requires serious hair, hair as helmet. Being so thickly anointed it is rarely ruffled, despite the vigour of the choreography but it may, from time to time, be fetchingly blown by a wind machine. There are lots of wind machines, and lots of chemical fog; although that hardly needs faking on a Mumbai film set, just open the window.

When recycled on television, the films have crawl-drum advertisements superimposed over them, top and bottom. The frames of the film are framed by ads for all categories of goods that glide by, like the famous newsflashes above Times Square:

THE P.K. HEALTH AND BEAUTY CLUB.

WANT INTERNET CONNECTION FREE?

Restaurants parade their menus. Details of hundreds of dishes pan by, while in the background, the chase continues as the Fonz pursues his inamorata.

BAILEY MINERAL WATER SERVED WITH THALI.

ICE-CREAM AND BOOKING HALL FACILITIES AVAILABLE FOR WEDDINGS AT REASONABLE RATES.

The leading men in India are all identical. Not only has India mastered the nuclear weapon but it is skilled at human cloning. As well as being high of hair the stars are invariably broad of shoulder, narrow of hip, proud of pectoral. Their noses aren't noses but prows and their eyes, when not hidden by dark glasses, are deep, dark and mysterious like the caves that consumed Miss Quested in *Passage to India*. While devastatingly dental (their teeth seem to have been carved from the finest elephant ivory) there is no hint of mental activity. And few hints of acting ability. The almost-lovers are invariably surrounded by a host of dancers, male and female, who cavort to choreography that is both rigorously regimented and defiantly unoriginal.

But at least this rubbish is Indian rubbish. And despite the popularity of the latest James Bond film, Indians still prefer Indian films and persist in attempting to hybridise and mutate imported idoms. Take MTV: a huge success on television around the rest of the planet, it sank like a stone on the subcontinent. You'll see telltale traces of Michael Jackson's dance routines in the local film clips, but not much Michael Jackson.

Gita Mehta told me of her 'hope, prayer and belief' that a billion Indian anarchists would take the homogeneity of America 'and put it through some sort of weird organic process and retain a heterogeneity and make of American homogeneity something which is peculiarly Indian in its heterogeneity'.

It's like the McDonald's franchises that are appearing in the major cities. A Big Mac is a Big Mac is a Big Mac, except that in India the beef has been replaced by a mutton patty. Here is a culture that has managed to accommodate the Muslims and the British. So it might, just might, cope with the Americans.

After a couple of hours' channel surfing, looking at a plethora of channels showing film clips of extended foreplay — of teasing sexual tension that, obeying the tantric, avoid climax — I stumble onto CNN, where the improbably entitled Elsa Klensh, a woman who seems to have an Australian accent, is giving us an overview of the Paris fashion shows.

After an hour of well-fleshed Fonzes chasing their voluptuous maidens through myriad locations, I find myself watching models, human exclamation marks, parading up and down catwalks stiff and unsmiling. Behold the zombies of haute couture, the walking corpses, the living dead.

We are now confronted by a model whose hair has been augmented with piles of tattered rope and what seems to be seaweed. This corpse has been dragged from the water. Others have their faces painted white to intensify their appeal to necrophiliacs. They have contact lenses that give them, of all things, red eyes, like the effects you get with bad flash photography. And what they're wearing are not so much garments as shrouds. The bodies wave and undulate, as though animation was struggling with rigor mortis.

Now the models have no hair at all. Their heads are shaven. This is the nastiest aspect of the fashion trade — fashism — not merely high camp but savagely misogynist. I return, with relief, to another luscious, fragrant fragment of Indian film. It is like replacing a mouthful of gravel with a packet of lollies.

There is, of course, another Indian film industry, one symbolised by the work of Satyajit Ray, the late, great Bengali filmmaker. When I met Ray decades ago he responded with joy and surprise to my declaration that Donskoi's *The Gorky Trilogy* headed my list of favourite films. 'But they were the very films that inspired me to make *The Apu Trilogy*!'

So it was prewar Russian films, rather than an Indian film or American films, that had been his inspiration. In the *Statesman*, the leading Calcutta English daily, he'd written in the late 1940s:

> It should be realised that the average American film is a bad model, if only because it depicts a way of life so utterly at variance with our own. Moreover the high technical polish which is the hallmark of the standard Hollywood product would be impossible to achieve under existing Indian conditions. What the Indian cinema needs today is not more gloss but more imagination, more integrity and a more intelligent appreciation of the limitation of the medium.

Ray would swim against the tide for the rest of his life, one of the few Indian filmmakers who found a significant international audience. This before he found a passionate local one. Thus *Pather Panchali*, the first part of *The Apu Trilogy*, was premiered at MOMA, the Museum of Modern Art in New York, where it was greatly honoured months before it was released in Calcutta.

Attempts were made to ban *Pather Panchali* from the Cannes festival. Indian bureaucrats found its portrait of poverty embarrassing. (To put this into context, Australia's Commonwealth Film Unit was just freeing itself of long-term prohibitions to admit to sharks, funnel-web spiders or poisonous reptiles.) But Nehru was moved by the film and gave it his personal endorsement.

Finally Ray got a distribution deal — the film would open in a chain of theatres in southern, central and northern Calcutta. Trained in advertising, Ray had designed five billboards for the film — each remarkable for its austerity. But the posters found an audience and the audience found themselves enraptured. 'The newspaper notices were full of adjectives praising the film,' Ray recalls in his diaries. 'Later the film was shown in other cities always without subtitles (because we had run out of funds) in spite of which it drew the same kind of response.'

But these days there seems to be little response to films such as Ray's. The low opinion of the gay film-maker in Mumbai seems to prevail. While there is an alternative cinema, one that wins praise at film festivals, the cinema of social protest is as marginalised in India as it is around the world. Everywhere, it seems, people prefer their films to be lies at twenty-four frames per second.

16

The Bomb

China is listened to. Even Russia, in its reduced circumstances, can still command attention. The Europeans have their place at the table of international affairs. But India?

India cannot understand why the world ignores it. Its ancient history, its massive population, its surging economy and its vast army should guarantee political clout. Yet it seems that the best known and most influential Indians are its novelists, not its politicians or diplomats. India is popular as a film location, as a tourist destination, as a place where the culturally cringing Westerners seek drugs and/or spiritual truth. But since Indira Gandhi's bold attempt to lead the non-aligned nations the world has not sought its counsel. Which is why there was a smell of cordite in the air even before the BJP had formed a government. The nuclear bomb had been the time bomb of Indian politics — and when the bombs began exploding in the desert they were India's way of banging loudly on the doors they believe have been slammed in their faces.

The one, two, three nuclear bombs that were detonated in the deserts of Rajistan echoed an event that first occurred in the deserts of Los Alamos just before dawn on 16 July 1945. This was the birthday of the bomb. And India was there, at least in spirit.

In his moral and political history of the atomic scientists, *Brighter than a Thousand Suns*, Dr Robert Jungk described the nuclear dawn:

During the ensuing period of waiting, which seemed an eternity, hardly a word was spoken. Everyone was giving free play to their thoughts. But so far as those who had been asked can remember, these thoughts were not apocalyptic. Most people concerned, it appears, were trying to work out how long it would be before they could shift their uncomfortable position and obtain some kind of view of the spectacle awaited. Fermi, experimentally-minded as ever, was holding scraps of paper, with which he meant to gauge the air pressure and thereby estimate the strength of the explosion the moment it occurred. Frisch was intent on memorising the phenomenon as precisely as possible, without allowing either excitement or preconceived notions to interfere with his faculties of perception. Groves was wondering for the hundredth time whether he had taken every possible step to ensure rapid evacuation in the case of a disaster. Oppenheimer oscillated between fears that the experiment would fail and fears that it would succeed.

Then everything happened faster than it could be understood. No one saw the first flash of the atomic fire itself. It was only possible to see its dazzling white reflection in the sky and on the hills. Those who then ventured to turn their heads perceived a bright ball of flame, growing steadily larger and larger. 'Good God, I believe that the long-haired boys have lost control!' a senior officer shouted. Carson Mark, one of the most brilliant members of the Theoretical Division, actually thought — though his intelligence told him the thing was impossible — that the ball of fire would never stop growing til it had enveloped all heaven and earth. At that moment everyone forgot what he had intended to do.

Groves wrote: 'Some of the men in their excitement, having had three years to get ready for it, at the last moment forgot those welders' helmets and stumbled out of the cars where they were sitting. They were blinded for two to three seconds. In that time they lost the view of what they had been waiting over three years to see.' People were transfixed with fright of the power of the explosion. Oppenheimer was clinging to one of the uprights in the control room. A passage from the Bhagavadgita, the sacred epic of the Hindus, flashed into his mind.

'If the radiance of a thousand suns
were to burst into the sky,
that would be like
the splendour of the Mighty One — '

Yet, when the sinister and gigantic cloud rose up in the far distance over point zero, he was reminded of another line from the same source ...

'I am become Death, the shatterer of worlds.'

Sri Krishna, the Exalted One, Lord of the fate of mortals, uttered the phrase. But Robert Oppenheimer was only a man, into whose hands a mighty, a far too mighty, power had been given.

It is a striking fact that none of those present reacted to the phenomenon so professionally as he had supposed he would. They all, even those — who constituted the majority — ordinarily without religious faith or even any inclination thereto, recounted their experience in words derived from the linguistic fields of myth and theology. GOLLANCZ 1958

India's nuclear program was, of course, an open secret, a boastful secret, like Israel's. But under pressure from the major players, from the nations that saw themselves as the nuclear Parsis, the keepers of the atomic flame, Delhi had abandoned testing, stopped boasting. It seemed as if the genie was back in the lamp. But the new government wanted, once more, to assert Krishna's pre-eminence — in a warning to Muslim Pakistan, to Communist China, to an arrogant Washington and, most ominously of all, to Muslim India.

The test sites became, in nanoseconds, the burning *ghats* for Gandhi's peaceful vision. Provoking the inevitable response from Pakistan, the subcontinent became, as was intended, the focus of world attention and, tragically, the location of yet another arms race that neither side could afford. Neither politically, nor economically. Yet the poor of India and Pakistan were seen dancing in the streets, exulting in, and exalting, the bomb.

Hindi is India's national language, spoken by more than 380 million in the north. Hindi newspapers sell 15 million copies a day, three times as many as English language dailies, and have a readership approaching 100 million. That's six times greater than their English rivals. Discounted by the urban elites as populist and sensational, the Hindi press is pretty good at catching the mood of the nation. Or, perhaps, at directing it. Thus they led the euphoria in the post-bomb bliss, and this was both echoed and amplified in the English papers. Nobody dared dissent.

I meet an old general, a Parsi, who had held high positions in previous governments. He'd witnessed the first of the Indian bomb tests, and his eyes shine as he remembered the day the nuclear fire was ignited. 'It was exciting,' he said, 'so very exciting.'

And once again, India was very excited.

When the first nuclear bomb was detonated at Los Alamos, only the inner sanctum of scientists was permitted to witness it, or even to know about it. But there was a problem, some people living near the experimental area — up to a distance of 200 kilometres away — had seen an unusually bright light in the sky around 5.30 am. They were provided with disinformation by the Manhattan Project's press agent: 'A munitions depot has blown up in the Alamogordo region. No lives have been lost.'

However, within a few days, the scientists' whispers had carried the news to all Manhattan Project laboratories.

Jungk continues the stories in *Brighter than a Thousand Suns*:

> Harrison Brown, one of the younger men on research at Oak Ridge, recalls: 'We knew all about the fireball, the mushroom cloud, the intense heat. Following Alamogordo many of us signed a petition urging that the atomic bomb should not be used against Japan without prior demonstration and opportunity to surrender. And we urged that the government start immediately to study the possibility of securing international control of the new weapon.

Already the other bombs, the other two of the original trinity, were on their way to Hiroshima and Nagasaki.

For a time mushroom explosions remained fashionable, ostentatious displays of military supremacy. But then human beings began to feel ashamed and afraid, and bomb tests went underground, out of sight. Where they were shrouded in millions of tonnes of earth as much as in secrecy. These implosions in the desert minimised political fallout as well as the wind-blown distribution of radiation.

When the Earth shook in Rajistan, great concavities appeared as the over-burden collapsed into the subterranean craters. While far less spectacular than the old-style tests, they were somehow more sinister. One feared for the world. But most of all one felt pity for the poor of the one-nation-that-might-have-been, the secular India that was torn apart by sectarianism half a century earlier, giving birth to Pakistan.

Of course, many more people died when India and Pakistan were born than in the bombing of Hiroshima and Nagasaki. And they were killed with knives, axes and clubs. You don't need nuclear weapons for mass slaughter — the Rwandan genocide was achieved with machetes. But to give history's greatest weapon to two peoples whose conflicts preceded nationhood, who have been waging war on each other for half the twentieth century, doesn't seem a particularly good idea.

Clearly the West's response to the Indian and Pakistani tests was an outburst of hypocrisy that dazzled like a thousand suns. The nations that had taken the world to the edge of the abyss, that had added megaton, overkill, and pre-emptive strike to the vocabulary, that had buried their missiles like dirty secrets in a thousand underground silos, or hidden them beneath the oceans in submarines, calling their strategy MAD (for Mutual Assured Destruction) were not in the best position to moralise about the decisions taken in New Delhi and Islamabad. Especially when the US, the Chinese and the Russian missiles were still aimed at each other's cities. And what of Britain's bombs? And France's? It's unlikely that they've been beaten into ploughshares.

Throughout India there was dancing in the street, the devout worshipping their god of choice, Krishna or Mohammed, in his nuclear raiment. We are brown men, but we have the white man's weapon. We are poor but we are mighty. We can no longer be colonised, or patronised. That's why the nuclear explosions detonated explosions of joy throughout the nation. Forgive us, Mahatma, but pacifism is passé. You need nuclear bombs to attract attention, to command respect.

One felt sorry for the poor President who had signed his

name in the visitors' book at the Hiroshima Museum, expressing his belief in the unparalleled evil of nuclear weaponry. The government we watched swearing Mr Vajpayee into office simply couldn't wait to flex its nuclear muscles.

India's other secret weapon, Arundahti Roy, the world's most beautiful novelist, author of *The God of Small Things*, attacked the god of very big things, and her voice carried far further than Beijing's. China protested that India, and Pakistan, had 'plunged Asia into a new wave of tension', echoing, word perfect, the sanctimonious statements of the US, the UK and, yes, of Australia. Arundahti Roy's words were more eloquent and elegant. She denounced nuclear weapons as 'anti-democratic, anti-human and outright evil ... if drinking Coke was Western culture, then what is the possession of the bomb? It was just the Westerners had a disease: we copied them.'

Roy's words, from an 8000-word essay titled *The End of the Imagination*, published in the Indian journal *Outlook*, made front-page news in the same newspapers that had, just weeks earlier, been rejoicing in the success of the bomb tests. And let it be said that no significant newspaper in the entire nation, irrespective of language or position on the political spectrum, had failed to welcome the news from the desert testing grounds.

Her warnings against a subcontinent with 'a suicide bomber psyche' dominated reports of two important international conferences where the nuclear issue would be discussed: the ASEAN Regional Forum in Manila and the South Asian Association for Regional Co-operation in Colombo.

Any attempt to count the diplomatic cost of the nuclear policy is, however, dwarfed by the accountancy exercise made necessary by the Asian financial crisis. As Mr Tan told the ASEAN Regional Forum, 'The crisis broke out ferociously and has caused such tremendous damage which is no less than that of a war.' But he also made the powerful point that there are clear links between economic crises and regional stability.

From bomb tests to cricket Tests. The goodwill built up by a lacklustre cricket team evaporated when, ever obedient to the US, Australia echoed their diplomatic pieties. Years of bridge-building by the Australia–India Committee were destroyed in a single diplomatic tantrum.

The West doesn't begin to understand India's need to be taken seriously. It's fine for novels by Indians to win the Booker Prize, as long as they're in English. It's flattering to have an Oscar-winning movie about Gandhi, albeit with an English actor in the lead. And there's a few bob in being seen as a theme park by those with befuddled views of Indian culture. But India would trade all that, and more, to be taken seriously in world affairs, to be respected as a major player rather than the most fashionably foreign and fantasmagorical of far away places.

A military attache tells me that the Indian armed services are not as significant as their numbers suggest. He's a Texan, and in Texas one of the most powerful insults is to describe someone as 'all Stetson, no cattle'. In Delhi he finds a similar expression to characterise one of the world's largest, most bureaucratised and, consequently, most ineffectual armies: 'This tiger is all tail and no teeth.' Well, the bomb tests represent very large fangs, which is why the tiger wagged its tail.

Yet another side to the story soon emerged. The jubilation in the streets was being overshadowed by second thoughts.

On Hiroshima Day 50,000 Japanese stood in silence, remembering the cataclysmic event that had destroyed its city and a multitude of people. And the envoys of India and Pakistan had to listen politely as the Japanese PM, Keizo Obuchi, berated their governments for the tit-for-tat testing. On that same day, in Calcutta alone, 400,000 Indians gathered to protest the tests. And over one hundred of India's senior scientists risked the censure of their government employer by signing petitions of protest.

While there were fewer protesters in Pakistan, a journalist in Islamabad told me that feelings were running just as high, particularly when retaliation from the IMF pushed the nation to the verge of bankruptcy. National reserves were down to US$500 million, the currency was in free fall, inflation was out of control and Pakistan was struggling to avoid default on its immense foreign debt.

In India there was evidence that the nuclear strategy had blown up in the BJP's face. Western commentators didn't seem to notice but the BJP did badly in subsequent by-elections. Then, after 100 days in office, the government took out a full-page ad in the major papers, the papers that had, without exception, printed approving, even exultant editorials supporting the tests. The purpose of the advertisement was to list the new government's 'eight proudest achievements'. Significantly, the nuclear blasts were not among them. Indeed, they rated just a passing mention in a caption to a photograph of Vajpayee.

The middle class were increasingly unhappy with the prospect of nuclear war. They realised that if conflict was to break out with Pakistan, or for that matter with China, the major cities would be among the primary targets and they'd be among the first to die. The idea of the orderly evacuation of a city such as Mumbai was, of course, laughable. A missile would take only three minutes to arrive — about the time it would take you to nose your car into the traffic on even the least congested of days.

Suddenly the hawks in India and Pakistan were making dove-like cooings and it seemed only a matter of time before both would profess their willingness to consider the appropriate international treaties. It was at this moment that the journalist P. Sainath came across a significant document. Not something with 'Top Secret' stamped all over it. Simply a poem written by Atal Bihari Vajpayee before he embarked on a prime ministerial and bomb-testing career.

For many years Vajpayee has written rhymes in the Hindi language. Apparently these caused excruciating pain to the nation's Hindi poets who point out that his verses had not appeared in any reputable anthology. However in 1995 he went public with a book of his own: *My 51 Poems*. As P. Sainath points out, this 'establishes conclusively that if he couldn't write poetry, at least he could count'.

The poem is called *Hiroshima ki Peedha*, and to give you a feeling for its rhythms here goes with the first two verses:

kisee raat ko
meree neend achanak uchat jaatee hai,
aankh khul jaatee hai,
mein sochne lagataa hoon ki
jin vaigyanikon ne aNu astron kaa
Aavishkaar kiyaa thaa:
ve Hiroshima-Nagasaki ke

bheeshan narsanhaar ke samaachaar sunkar,
raat ko soye kaise honge?

daatn mein phansaa tinkaa,
aankh ki kirkiree,
paavn mein chubha kaatnaa,
aankhon ki neend,
man ka chain udaa dete hain.

And now, a translation of the entire text.

The Pain of Hiroshima

Some nights
my sleep is suddenly disturbed,
my eyes open,
and I think that
those scientists who invented
atomic weapons:
When they heard the news of
the terrible genocide of Hiroshima-Nagasaki,
how did they sleep at night?

A speck in the teeth, a mote in the eyes,
a thorn stuck in the feet,
take the sleep from my eyes,
my peace of mind.

The death of a relative,
the demise of a loved one,
the passing of an acquaintance,
in fact even the parting of a pet animal,
fill the heart with such pain, such sorrow that,
sleep does not come, even on trying.
From side to side, turning all night.

But the inventors
of that ultimate weapon
which, on the dark night of the sixth of August, 1945,
danced the dance of death in Hiroshima-Nagasaki

and took the sacrifice of over 200,000 people,
crippled thousands of people for life.

Did they, for a second even,
get the feeling that what they had done
was not right?
If so, then time will not put them in the dock,
but if not then history will never
forgive them.

17

Conclusion

While our countries have human histories stretching back to the time before man measured time, both India and Australia are recent additions to the rollcall of nations. Our institutions reflect a similar colonial heritage and generations of British rule. Our national capitals, Canberra and New Delhi, date from the same era. Both shaped by single and singular men, architects from the northern hemisphere, they are still warm from the kiln.

With baking hinterlands, both nations have populations that cling to a coastline. Dorothy Mackellar's sunburnt country with its sweeping plains, far horizons, jewelled seas and flooding rains could just as well serve as an anthem for India.

So much for similarities. The essential difference, it seems to me, lies in the fact that the Australian journey has us trying to walk in the middle of the road whereas the choking traffic of Indian history is chaotic and conflictive. We aspire to moderation to such an extent that even our extremes are timid. More than middle of the road we are middle-class and middle-brow.

Neither rural nor urban, we are a suburban people and, a few brave souls sipping coffee on the footpaths not withstanding, we live our private lives privately. Behind venetians. Looking at electronic neighbours on television.

CONCLUSION 221

India is not a suburban country. Nor do their people aspire to privacy. Whether enduring the impossible densities of the cities or as one of the half billion people living in rural villages, life there is unapologetically public.

Even Australian religious observations, such as they are, are hidden from view. We are, by and large, faintly embarrassed by faith. While we might tick the Anglican or Roman Catholic box on the census form, we are an agnostic people who cannot begin to comprehend the passions of Indian belief. The extremes are everywhere. On the one hand, India suffocates in the power of superstitions. On the other, the nation has a gift for nuclear physics and computer science.

While we strive to be moderate, India is exultantly immoderate, taking everything to the limit. Extremism finds physical form in the geography of the Himalayas contrasting with the deserts of Rajasthan, just as it was embodied in the wealth of the maharajahs compared to the destitution of the casteless. Though the royal titles are gone and the palaces are either ruins or dilapidated museums, the economic contrasts endure. In a land of a million millionaires there are half a billion who are lucky to reach that milestone in nutrition, the all-important 2000 calories a day.

Yes, Australia does have Kerry Packer and, from time to time, Rupert Murdoch. But tycoons like Kerry are freaks created by statistics. (Someone has to be the tallest, the oldest, the fattest, the richest.) Our tycoons show up a growing disparity between rich and poor, but are the rule-proving exceptions that emphasise, yet again, the comparative flatness of our economic landscape.

We Australians agonise over whether or not we are racists. (That such a debate is necessary suggests that we are.) But deeper than that, Australians are differencists. We are embarrassed by difference in any form — by disability or by eccentricity, whereas the social and cultural dynamics of India produce differences as surely as the pressure of tectonic plates pile up the mountain peaks.

Just as their traffic jams make our city streets seem deserted, India's technicolour makes us seem monochromatic. Where Indians are theatrical, we are more comfortable sitting in the audience. If Jews are, as Arthur Koestler said, 'the exposed nerve ends of mankind', Indians are mankind at its most intense. They are a people who find ecstasy in everything from their dancing gods to death itself.

India is humanity without inhibition, without apology.